AMY ANDREWS

2017

A BOOK OF GRACE-FILLED DAYS

LOYOLA PRESS.
A JESUIT MINISTRY

Chicago

LOYOLA PRESS.
A JESUIT MINISTRY

3441 N. Ashland Avenue
Chicago, Illinois 60657
(800) 621-1008
www.loyolapress.com

Cover and interior design by Kathy Kikkert.

ISBN-13: 978-0-8294-4397-4
ISBN-10: 0-8294-4397-5
Library of Congress Control Number: 2016939171

Printed in the United States of America.

16 17 18 19 20 21 22 Bang 10 9 8 7 6 5 4 3 2 1

INTRODUCTION

This is a book about grace, so I want to begin by sharing a little of my own story, how I first encountered grace. I'm not sure this story would be as fresh in my mind if it weren't for Frances Hodgson Burnett's *The Secret Garden*, which I read to my children this past year. The book tells the story of three children who find God in a garden. I read it and reread it as a child, but I had forgotten why. In the past few weeks as the book unfolded, I was stunned to see a description reminiscent of the beginnings of my own faith.

When I was born my mother planted a tree. I doubt I much noticed its progress for years, but nevertheless we were both growing, and then one day there it was, as if it had always been waiting for me. And I parted its long curtain of leaves and walked into that little, glowing-green sanctuary of branches and learned how to climb its trunk. I was not raised with any sort of explicit religious faith, but my parents loved me, and to me the garden was just another extension of their love. I spent a good part of my childhood there, watching birds, hiding under the pines, taming a chipmunk, and climbing to the top of my weeping cherry. It was there I first felt myself alone before God, his presence seemingly in the stars or the whispering tree. When I prayed, some natural child's prayer, I prayed perched in the highest branches with night or sun on my face.

Near the end of *The Secret Garden*, which up to that point makes virtually no mention of God, there is an almost ecstatic scene. The three children stand in the garden, which had once seemed dead but is now alive, and are suddenly so overcome with joy they want to sing out. So Dickon, the one who charms animals and flowers, tells them to take off their hats and then teaches them how to sing the doxology, beginning "Praise God from whom all blessings flow . . ." When they finish, the other boy, Colin, is perplexed. All along he'd been calling the garden and its mysterious life-giving properties "the Magic." "Perhaps [this song] means just what I mean when I want to shout out that I am thankful to the Magic," he says. "Perhaps they are both the same thing. How can we know the exact names of everything?"

When I look back on it, the tree in my garden seems like a hand holding me up to heaven. It could have been the hand of my mother, who loved me more than herself and wanted to give me beauty, or it could have been the hand of God, who holds each one of us. But the way I look at things now,

I don't have to choose. For how do we know the exact names of everything? That tree was both of their hands at once and also its own, bark-clad self.

I found faith in a garden. And later that early encounter led me to seek God out in churches. But even now as a Catholic, I have felt the need to return again and again to that original, natural experience. In our secular world it is so easy for us to compartmentalize our faith and either shrink down the name of God, trapping it within churches, or else collapse everything into that name until nothing else matters. But instead the name of God should spread out, infuse the world with mystery and grace, making everything matter, and we should look for it everywhere, not just at the altar but in soup kitchens and fields and faces.

So for me, writing this book became such a search. This search took me out into the world beyond the explicit domain of religion and into the books I've read, the places I've seen, and the sorrows and joys I've lived. But more often than not this search took me into Scripture itself, trying to see it not as a dead thing but as something that comes alive and still has meaning and power for us today. Stories begin to "live" only when we enter them, so by entering the stories of my own life and of Scripture, I wanted to find the Word of God living both in and outside the Good Book. We cannot know the exact names of things, as Colin said, but in them we can look for the One from whom all blessings flow. So come with me and search through Scripture and our days, through both the mundane and the glorious, the joyful and the tragic, for grace, which is known by many names but is here among us nonetheless, sure as the sun.

Sunday

NOVEMBER 27

• FIRST SUNDAY OF ADVENT •

In days to come,
the mountain of the LORD'S house
shall be established as the highest mountain
and raised above the hills.
—ISAIAH 2:2

I love thinking of the Lord's house as a mountain. The author
Annie Dillard once wrote, "Mountains are giant, restful,
absorbent. You can heave your spirit into a mountain and the
mountain will keep it, folded." Sometimes that is exactly how
it feels, that if I am going to unburden myself at all, I will
have to heave my spirit like a great, weighty thing. But it
helps to imagine that restful presence waiting for the catch,
and then holding my spirit, folded, until I am ready to bear it
again. In the days to come, as we learn to wait, it might be
easier if we first lighten our loads. So heave whatever weighs
you down into the mountain. Don't worry; it will keep.

Isaiah 2:1–5
Psalm 122:1–2,3–4,4–5,6–7,8–9
Romans 13:11–14
Matthew 24:37–44

⇒ 1 ⇐

Lord, I am not worthy to have you enter under my roof.
—MATTHEW 8:8

The poet Mary Oliver writes in an Advent poem that she has swept and washed, but still nothing in her house is as shining as it should be for the Lord. She describes all the creatures who are thwarting her efforts at perfection. There are mice nesting under the sink, squirrels gnawing ragged entrances, dogs snoring on the floor. She can't turn them away. But in the end she realizes that she's been speaking to the Lord all morning and afternoon whenever she's said, "Come in, come in." Regardless of the state of your house, shining or unkempt, it was not meant to be empty. This Advent, find a way to say, "Come in."

Isaiah 4:2–6
Psalm 122:1–2,3–4b,4cd–5,6–7,8–9
Matthew 8:5–11

NOVEMBER 29

*Although you have hidden these things from the wise and the learned
you have revealed them to the childlike.*

—LUKE 10:21

St. Jerome tells us that when St. John the Evangelist had
grown very old, he had to be carried to church and could
barely speak. All he ever said was, "Little children, love one
another." His disciples eventually asked him, "Master, why do
you keep on saying this?" And John answered simply,
"Because it is a precept of the Lord, and it is sufficient if this
alone is done." We are called to be like children. Don't make
the central task of life more complicated than it is.

Isaiah 11:1–10
Psalm 72:1–2,7–8,12–13,17
Luke 10:21–24

The command of the LORD is clear,
enlightening the eye.
—PSALM 19:9

The nature photographer Richard Gottardo made a short
time-lapse clip of clouds rolling into the Rocky Mountains.
The clouds look like ghosts, leaping about, and sometimes
like great blankets of solid fog. At one point you can see the
sun blazing behind the ghosts, almost breaking through but
not quite. Today the psalm tells us that the command of the
Lord is clear, as if it is always evident what God wants and
what we are supposed to do. But really, this is only how it
should be, not how it is. Instead, God's command comes to
us more like that veiled sun, always there behind the
darkness, behind our ghosts, bearing down until we finally
manage to see.

Romans 10:9–18
Psalm 19:8,9,10,11
Matthew 4:18–22

Thursday

DECEMBER 1

*The rain fell, the floods came,
and the winds blew and buffeted the house.*
—MATTHEW 7:25

You know what comes next. It's like that old folktale: the
wolf huffs and puffs and blows the house down, and the little
pig is eaten up. Complete and total ruin. Folktales tell us
what we already know. With a few grim plot points, they
sum up the stark consequences of our actions. But the stories
Jesus tells are never just folktales. Jesus redeems our stories,
completing them not with ruin but with Resurrection. Out of
love, he warns us to be like the wise man and build our house
on rock, but he knows that we will fail and that he will have
to come, again and again, into the ruin of our house and help
us raise it up once more. So take heart and build.

Isaiah 26:1–6
Psalm 118:1 and 8–9,19–21,25–27a
Matthew 7:21,24–27

DECEMBER 2

*Wait for the LORD with courage;
be stouthearted, and wait for the LORD.*
—PSALM 27:14

Usually when we wait, we need merely patience to sit and do
nothing until our name is called. Advent is the season of
waiting. But the word itself, which comes from the Latin
adventus, means "the approach or arrival of the gods"; it means
"epiphany." Will patience get us through to this great
encounter, the arrival of God? When I was waiting for my
second child to be born after having lost my first to stillbirth,
waiting was all I did. But if someone had told me to be
patient I would have screamed. I never sat quietly. Every
second of every day I willed clocks to tick and hearts to beat.
Waiting was almost unbearable. It wasn't just patience I
needed but courage, to be stouthearted and wait for
the Lord.

Isaiah 29:17–24
Psalm 27:1,4,13–14
Matthew 9:27–31

DECEMBER 3

Without cost you have received; without cost you are to give.
—MATTHEW 10:8

"We live in a time when almost everything can be bought,"
writes the Harvard professor Michael Sandel. "Over the past
three decades, markets—and market values—have come to
govern our lives as never before." More and more I find
myself trying to solve a problem with a product. But this
frantic casting about for commercial solutions will never get
to the heart of things. Next time, before turning to Amazon
or eBay, those great modern oracles, ask yourself, "How can I
solve my problems without cost? What can I give that
isn't bought?"

Isaiah 30:19–21,23–26
Psalm 147:1–2,3–4,5–6
Matthew 9:35–10:1,5a,6–8

Sunday

DECEMBER 4

There shall be no harm or ruin on all my holy mountain;
for the earth shall be filled with knowledge of the LORD,
as water covers the sea.
—ISAIAH 11:9

I often think about the seabed, how it seems like another
planet but how it's really just earth covered by water. It has
chasms and vast plains, cliffs and hill country. Up here above
sea level, there's also a layer that covers everything, which
scientists call the boundary layer. It's where the wind blows,
temperatures fluctuate, and people live, yet we don't
experience it as anything more than air. Lord, we let your
knowledge brush past us as if it were air. No wonder you
once covered the earth with water. But help us to feel it even
now as we breathe, so that no harm or ruin will come on
your holy mountain that holds us above the flood.

Isaiah 11:1–10
Psalm 72:1–2,7–8,12–13,17
Romans 15:4–9
Matthew 3:1–12

DECEMBER 5

*The desert and the parched land will exult;
the steppe will rejoice and bloom.*
—ISAIAH 35:1

These lines from Isaiah make me think of a set of questions
by the poet Eugene Warren: "Is it chance / or dance moves /
the world?" he asks. "Is the world / blind and dumb / or
bloom, festal? A vain jest, / or holy feast?" These are Advent
questions. In Advent we contemplate more explicitly the
doubts that always haunt us. Is God really there? Is there
really any meaning? Will He really come? I have asked these
questions a thousand times. But today Isaiah takes pity on our
doubt and cries out the answer: the desert will bloom with
abundant flowers and rejoice with joyful song.

Isaiah 35:1–10
Psalm 85:9ab and 10,11–12,13–14
Luke 5:17–26

DECEMBER 6

• ST. NICHOLAS, BISHOP •

The grass withers, the flower wilts,
when the breath of the LORD blows upon it.
—ISAIAH 40:7

God is paradox. Yesterday flowers bloomed in the desert;
today they die in the fields. And even worse, they wither
with the Lord's breath. But maybe that is not so shocking.
God is not just in heaven but in everything—the soil, the
water, the air. Flowers die because they live, and all living
things must die. So what are we to do? Give up on
yesterday's song because we know what's coming? God is
paradox but he also resolves paradox. The passage in Isaiah
ends like this: "Though the grass withers and the flower wilts,
the word of our God stands forever." God's breath in
December is cold. Death is coming. But so is the Incarnation,
when the eternal Word of God will become flesh and dwell
among us and lend his life to ours.

Isaiah 40:1–11
Psalm 96:1–2,3 and 10ac,11–12,13
Matthew 18:12–14

⇒ 10 ⇐

DECEMBER 7

• ST. AMBROSE, BISHOP AND DOCTOR OF THE CHURCH •

*Take my yoke upon you and learn from me,
for I am meek and humble of heart;
and you will find rest for yourselves.*
—MATTHEW 11:29

It used to be that books were always read out loud. The first recorded instance of a silent reader is St. Augustine's description of St. Ambrose. "As he read," says Augustine, "his eyes glanced over the pages and his heart searched out the sense, but his voice and tongue were silent." Today, reading silently is old hat. Even so, I'm not sure the kind of reading Ambrose did is that common. We read in the midst of noise, skimming the lines. It strikes me as humble to read like Ambrose, to allow someone else's words to command your time and heart for a while. Augustine says Ambrose found rest this way, "free from the clamor of other men's business." Today, step back from the clamor and read with humble attention.

Isaiah 40:25–31
Psalm 103:1–2,3–4,8 and 10
Matthew 11:28–30

Thursday

DECEMBER 8

• THE IMMACULATE CONCEPTION OF THE BLESSED VIRGIN MARY,
PATRONAL FEASTDAY OF THE UNITED STATES OF AMERICA •

*He chose us in him, before the foundation of the world, to be holy and
without blemish before him.*
—EPHESIANS 1:4

Immaculate is one of those words that smacks of
perfectionism. A house without dust. Skin without blemish.
Life without a wrinkle. Do we really want to strive for these
perfections, which seem so counter to accepting who we are
and how life is? But immaculate is used today in a very
specific sense to mean "without sin." Yet sin is just another
heavy, guilt-inducing term, which can lead to perfectionism.
So what if instead, when we think of sin, we don't think of
this or that imperfection but of what keeps us alienated from
ourselves and others and God? Today we renew our belief
that we were created to live, as Mary was, without these
barriers, to let God slowly grow inside of us, until God is all
in all, and we are no longer alone.

Genesis 3:9–15,20
Psalm 98:1,2–3ab,3cd–4 (1a)
Ephesians 1:3–6,11–12
Luke 1:26–38

⇒ 12 ⇐

Friday

DECEMBER 9

"We played the flute for you, but you did not dance,
we sang a dirge but you did not mourn."
—MATTHEW 11:17

My church in Chicago hosts local artists, giving them space to work and often an audience. Last week the theater troupe in residence hosted what they called a "theater experience." I took my children. We pounded on djembe drums, danced with giant painted puppets, and worked the sides of a huge parachute. But the climax was when our pastor stepped through a column of smoke to lead everyone in a line dance. The experience wasn't explicitly religious, but maybe because our pastor was there, or because the day was so joyful, the whole thing felt like a holy pageant. I left with aching muscles. How often do we ever dance? And for that matter, how often do we mourn? And yet they are there in every Mass, the dance and the dirge, calling our bodies and hearts to wake up.

Isaiah 48:17–19
Psalm 1:1–2,3,4 and 6
Matthew 11:16–19

DECEMBER 10

You were taken aloft in a whirlwind of fire,
in a chariot with fiery horses.
—SIRACH 48:9

I remember watching the racehorse American Pharoah win
the Triple Crown. And I couldn't help it, my heart was in my
throat as I watched him thunder down that last bit of track. I
tried to remember all the gambling and obscene fortune that
attends this sport, but I couldn't make any of it matter. Now I
am watching the phenomenon that is LeBron James in the
NBA playoffs. Again there is opulence, gambling, absurd
celebrity, yet I can't squelch that longing in me to get a
glimpse of a god. And apparently I'm not alone. The
stadiums are filled not with millionaires or people who stand
to win or lose but supplicants, holding their breath, hoping
to see a whirlwind of fire, a chariot with fiery horses, glory
incarnate.

Sirach 48:1–4,9–11
Psalm 80:2ac and 3b,15–16,18–19
Matthew 17:9a,10–13

The LORD God keeps faith forever.
—PSALM 146:6

To keep faith means not to break a promise. I've been reading *The Secret Garden* with my children. In it there's this wild boy of the English moors who is known as Dickon. He seems like St. Francis, taming animals and full of compassion and humility. "The most magic boy in the world," someone says of him. "He's like an angel." In many ways he's Christlike. At one point he's called upon to keep a secret. "If tha' was a missel thrush an' showed me where thy nest was, does tha' think I would tell anyone? Not me," he says in broad Yorkshire. "Tha' art as safe as a missel thrush." Lord, you keep faith forever. Even though we are stranded here in this life, the world as wild as a moor, we are as safe as a missel thrush with you.

Isaiah 35:1–6a,10
Psalm 146:6–7,8–9,9–10
James 5:7–10
Matthew 11:2–11

DECEMBER 12

• OUR LADY OF GUADALUPE •

I am coming to dwell among you.
—ZECHARIAH 2:14

The day Juan Diego first saw Our Lady of Guadalupe, she was right there, shimmering and glorious on a dusty hill. But that moment was so earth shattering that even decades later I bet he could still see her shining in his mind. And maybe the image was so bright that it felt less like memory and more like ongoing presence. This must be how it is to see from the vantage of eternity, everything still as it was. Very few will ever have a vision of Mary flaming on a hilltop, and yet God comes to all of us in stunning ways. What moments—births or deaths or chance bits of time—dwell in your mind, convincing you of eternity? As it says in Numbers, what in your life do you see, though not now? What do you behold, though not near?

Zechariah 2:14–17 or
Revelation 11:19a; 12:1–6a,10ab
Judith 13:18bcde,19
Luke 1:26–38 or 1:39–47

DECEMBER 13

• ST. LUCY, VIRGIN AND MARTYR •

I will bless the LORD at all times;
his praise shall ever be in my mouth.
—PSALM 34:2

Every year we go to a Santa Lucia festival and walk through
the streets at nightfall behind a girl with candles in her hair,
singing, "Night walks with heavy step, round yard and
hearth. As the sun departs from earth, shadows are brooding.
There in our dark house, walking with lit candles, Santa
Lucia, Santa Lucia!" We are called to bless the Lord at all
times, even when shadows are brooding, even when the
heavy steps of night walk in our house. But the saints help us,
for even when all seems lost, there they suddenly are,
blazing, proclaiming that the light has not gone out.

Zephaniah 3:1–2,9–13
Psalm 34:2–3,6–7,17–18,19 and 23
Matthew 21:28–32

I am the LORD, there is no other;
I form the light, and create the darkness.
I make well-being and create woe.
—ISAIAH 45:6–7

The perennial stumbling block to faith is the question, how could a good God create evil? And here is God himself confessing to the crime. So how are we as believers to make sense of this? A couple of things help me to do so. First, God says he *forms* light, *makes* well-being. *Forming* and *making* sound so physical, like the work of God's hands. Darkness and woe only come later, as if they are created as by-products of the real work. Second, when God says he creates darkness, he's not speaking about physics. After all, starlight fills even the outermost regions of space. By *darkness* he means instead our perception of darkness, for as St. John of the Cross said, "Faith is a dark night for man, but in this very way it gives him light."

Isaiah 45:6b–8,18,21b–25
Psalm 85:9ab and 10,11–12,13–14
Luke 7:18b–23

DECEMBER 15

O LORD, you brought me up from the nether world;
you preserved me from among those going down into the pit.
—PSALM 30:4

Salvation from death has been the hope of all people, in all times. It lies at the heart of much mythology. In the Nordic myth of Baldur the Beautiful, the god Baldur dies, and his mother rides weeping into Hel and begs for his life. His redemption is granted on the condition that every being and every last thing will grieve for his life. This is almost accomplished but for a dry snake of sin curled in a recess of rock who refuses to weep. With this failure, Baldur is kept below and his mother left to mourn. *O Lord*, the myths cry out, with a voice as big as history, *lift my life from the grave!* And here we are in Advent, waiting again for the one who will finally have a voice big enough to answer: *I am the Resurrection and the Life.*

Isaiah 54:1–10
Psalm 30:2 and 4,5–6,11–12a and 13b
Luke 7:24–30

May God have pity on us and bless us;
may he let his face shine upon us.
—PSALM 67:2

Here God is like the sun, shining down upon us. In other versions of this Old Testament blessing, it says, "May the Lord lift up his countenance." I love the combination of these translations, one looking down, the other looking up. It reminds me of this beautiful passage from the writer G. K. Chesterton: "Any agnostic or atheist whose childhood has known a real Christmas has ever afterwards, whether he likes it or not, an association in his mind between two ideas that most of mankind must regard as remote from each other; the idea of a baby and the idea of unknown strength that sustains the stars." Glory and humility, God's face looking down and up. This Advent, may the Lord's face shine down upon you and may he lift up his countenance and give you peace.

Isaiah 56:1–3a,6–8
Psalm 67:2–3,5,7–8
John 5:33–36

DECEMBER 17

Eleazar became the father of Matthan,
Matthan the father of Jacob,
Jacob the father of Joseph, the husband of Mary.
Of her was born Jesus who is called the Christ.
—MATTHEW 1:15–16

Last year during our Advent Lessons, Lights, and Carols service, the priest read the genealogy of Christ. You'd think a list of forty-one names would make for a pretty dull liturgy, but for me it was the highpoint. He read it in sections. At regular intervals, between prayers and songs, there'd come a timpani roll from the choir loft, and then a few generations of names, each one pronounced gravely, as if recognizing a death. It felt like that, like a funeral for everyone. And it would have felt hopeless, but at some point the last drum roll came, and with it the sudden, shocking appearance not of yet another who would die and be gone but of Jesus who is called the Christ.

Genesis 49:2,8–10
Psalm 72:1–2,3–4ab,7–8,17
Matthew 1:1–17

DECEMBER 18

And they shall name him Emmanuel,
which means "God is with us."
—MATTHEW 1:23

The word *with* first meant "against" or "opposed." But it shifted to mean "alongside" or "near." And as time went on the sense of proximity intensified, and eventually the word came to indicate "accompaniment" and even "union." "In the beginning was the Word, and the Word was with God, and the Word was God. He was in the beginning with God." And now God is *with* us. I don't know how we could ever make sense of this absurdly grand claim if it weren't for Mary who was with child. Mary shows us through her body how it might be possible to have a union between two things we'd once have thought were opposed.

Isaiah 7:10–14
Psalm 24:1–2,3–4,5–6 (7c and 10b)
Romans 1:1–7
Matthew 1:18–24

DECEMBER 19

When [Zechariah] came out, he was unable to speak to them,
and they realized that he had seen a vision in the sanctuary.
—LUKE 1:22

In one of Gerard Manley Hopkins's earliest poems, he commands his own voice and each of his senses to be still. Everything pales, he thinks, compared to what we'll someday experience in the golden streets. "Shape nothing, lips," he writes, "be lovely-dumb." I imagine it was like that for Zechariah. The vision in the sanctuary struck him lovely-dumb. What words would suffice? He walked about in glory, saying nothing. In contemplative prayer we close our eyes, follow the breath, bring fingertip to fingertip. "Shape nothing, lips. Be shellèd, eyes." As we retreat into silence, we actually gain a brighter sense of reality. But even this is only a shadow of what is to come.

Judges 13:2–7,24–25a
Psalm 71:3–4a,5–6ab,16–17
Luke 1:5–25

DECEMBER 20

Then the angel departed from her.
—LUKE 1:38

I've often thought about the angel coming to Mary. Our feasts and songs and icons celebrate the Annunciation. But I'd never thought about the moment when it was all over. I can only imagine it was something like what writer Annie Dillard experienced when she looked out on what she imagined was a field of angels. "I stood in pieces," she writes, "afraid I was unable to move. Something had unhinged the world." Later she describes the grave and stricken silence, the "unbearable green" and the "God-blasted, paralyzed" fields. People always comment on the bravery of Mary's yes. I never quite understood this. Wouldn't anyone say yes to an angel? But it seems unspeakably brave when I picture that later moment, when Mary stood before the God-blasted, paralyzed day and watched the angel depart.

Isaiah 7:10–14
Psalm 24:1–2,3–4ab,5–6
Luke 1:26–38

> *O my dove in the clefts of the rock,*
> *in the secret recesses of the cliff,*
> *Let me see you,*
> *let me hear your voice,*
> *For your voice is sweet,*
> *and you are lovely.*
> —SONG OF SONGS 2:14

Before I became a parent, I remember watching the British series *Seven Up!* and being struck by how one man described parenthood. It was the joyous physicality, he said, that surprised him, how much he loved his sons' bodies and smells. Later, I remember smelling my own children's infant breath and curling up with them pressed naked against my skin. The physical expression of love blurs with experience. Now I ask my husband to place his hands on my face as my mother once did. The Song of Songs is God's love song to us. And it makes sense that God will come to us in all that fullness, as sweet and lovely as a parent, a lover, a child.

Song of Songs 2:8–14 or Zephaniah 3:14–18a
Psalm 33:2–3,11–12,20–21
Luke 1:39–45

DECEMBER 22

My soul proclaims the greatness of the Lord;
my spirit rejoices in God my savior,
for he has looked upon his lowly servant.
—LUKE 1:46

I struggle all the time to find even a desire for worship.
Here's one trick I use to bring myself around. I think of an
experience I once had of glory. Up on a high mountain, I
looked out upon a great piece of our earth—sky, peaks,
streaks of light and cloud—glory unloosed from any
doctrine. Then I think about the look in my father's eyes
when he once sat by my hospital bed, or my mother's hands
on my face. And then I try to bring these images together: I
picture that great sky looking upon me with the eyes of my
father, brushing my cheeks with the hands of my mother.
God has looked upon what is lowly. The glory of heaven has
come down.

1 Samuel 1:24–28
1 Samuel 2:1,4–5,6–7,8abcd
Luke 1:46–56

Yes, he is coming, says the LORD *of hosts.*
But who will endure the day of his coming?
—MALACHI 3:1–2

This whole passage in Malachi is full of foreboding. "Who will endure the day of his coming?" "Who can stand when he appears?" As I read it I'm waiting to hear what terrible thing we'll be asked to bear. The prophet will come, it says, "to turn the hearts of the fathers to their children, and the hearts of the children to their fathers." *Is that all?* I think. But then I notice that I'm sitting here writing with the din of children running through my house. I scream for everyone to be quiet. The phone rings. The house is a wreck. I read the passage again. Who can stand when he appears? Who can turn their hearts when they should be turned?

Malachi 3:1–4,23–24
Psalm 25:4–5ab,8–9,10 and 14
Luke 1:57–66

Saturday

DECEMBER 24

In the tender compassion of our God
the dawn from on high shall break upon us,
to shine on those who dwell in darkness
and the shadow of death,
and to guide our feet into the way of peace.
—LUKE 1:78–79

There is a poem by Ford Madox Ford in which he imagines
heaven. At one point, God comes as "a man of great stature /
In a great cloak" to where the narrator is sitting at a table.
"Yet he never looked at us," writes Ford, "knowing that would
be such a joy as must be over-great for hearts that needed
quiet." It is the last day of Advent. Our wait is almost over.
Are we ready? In his tender compassion God will break
gently upon us like the dawn. He will give us who have quiet
hearts, who dwell in darkness, time to adjust.

2 Samuel 7:1–5,8b–12,14a,16
Psalm 89:2–3,4–5,27 and 29
Luke 1:67–79

⇒ 28 ⇐

DECEMBER 25

• THE NATIVITY OF THE LORD (CHRISTMAS) •

They name him Wonder-Counselor, God-Hero,
Father-Forever, Prince of Peace.
—ISAIAH 9:5

Kenning is the name for a compound noun, a metaphoric device often found in Old English poetry. Fire was called "bane of wood," sea was "whale-path," and sun, "sky-candle." We still stumble across the word *ken*, which means "beyond knowledge." Today in Isaiah, we have four kennings for the Lord. Each pairs something of this world—counselor, hero, father, prince—with something divine—wonder, God, forever, peace. And God would have always remained beyond our ken if it weren't for the Incarnation, when he joined man to God, sorrow to Comforter, and life to Redeemer.

VIGIL:
Isaiah 62:1–5
Psalm 89:4–5,16–17,27,29 (2a)
Acts 13:16–17,22–25
Matthew 1:1–25 or 1:18–25

DAWN:
Isaiah 62:11–12
Psalm 97:1,6,11–12
Titus 3:4–7
Luke 2:15–20

MIDNIGHT:
Isaiah 9:1–6
Psalm 96:1–2,2–3,11–12,13
Titus 2:11–14
Luke 2:1–14

DAY:
Isaiah 52:7–10
Psalm 98:1,2–3,3–4,5–6 (3c)
Hebrews 1:1–6
John 1:1–18 or 1:1–5,9–14

They will hand you over to courts and scourge you in their synagogues.
—MATTHEW 10:17

Even though I have largely given up on historical arguments for the Resurrection, all those attempts to skirt faith, I still find the testimony of the early Christians so compelling. The theologian N. T. Wright says that it was those who believed in bodily Resurrection, that dangerous claim that death is defeated, who were burned at the stake and thrown to the lions. It wasn't that they believed in Jesus; the Gnostics were left alone. It was that they believed he rose. If the Resurrection had not happened, would they have given up their lives so blithely? Would they have still been overcome with love, as St. Stephen was, even as stones were flying, and prayed for God not to punish their enemies?

Acts 6:8–10; 7:54–59
Psalm 31:3cd–4,6 and 8ab,16bc and 17
Matthew 10:17–22

DECEMBER 27

• ST. JOHN, APOSTLE AND EVANGELIST •

What was from the beginning,
what we have heard,
what we have seen with our eyes,
what we looked upon
and touched with our hands.
—1 JOHN 1:1

The reading for today starts with a breathless litany of beginnings. John stammers away trying to get something out, and if you skip ahead to today's Gospel reading you'll see why. John "ran faster than Peter and arrived at the tomb first." He went in, and "he saw and believed." And what did he see? One of my parish priests answered this so simply: he saw nothing. Later John hears, looks upon, touches, but already he believed. And thank God for that, for we are like John at the tomb. That nothing is all we've got. That and the stammering voice of John begging us to believe his account.

1 John 1:1–4
Psalm 97:1–2,5–6,11–12
John 20:1a and 2–8

DECEMBER 28

• THE HOLY INNOCENTS, MARTYRS •

Rise, take the child and his mother, flee to Egypt,
and stay there until I tell you.
Herod is going to search for the child to destroy him.
—MATTHEW 2:13

Today is Childermas, or Holy Innocents' Day, a remembering of the infants Herod slayed, the very first martyrs. But the day itself has an odd history. It eventually became a day for merrymaking, pranks, and children ruling the roost. For a time it even got caught up in the Medieval Feast of Fools, when everyone would mock religious ritual. In England, attempting to regain the proper mournfulness of the day, parents began whipping children in their beds in the morning. But to me, merrymaking seems appropriate on a day meant for children. Children don't stay with grief the way we do; they are too present, too quick to laugh. So today, try listening to the haunting "Coventry Carol"—"All young children to slay, Lully, lullay"—and watch children dance, even as you weep.

1 John 1:5–2:2
Psalm 124:2–3,4–5,7b–8
Matthew 2:13–18

DECEMBER 29

*Whoever keeps his word,
the love of God is truly perfected in him.*
—1 JOHN 2:5

Today we continue celebrating the martyrs, in particular
St. Thomas Becket. When I think of Becket, I see Richard
Burton from the movie *Becket*. He is depicted as a Norman
orphan who became the wenching and drinking partner of
King Henry and his right-hand man. He even remains loyal
when King Henry brings about the suicide of Becket's wife.
"So long as Becket must improvise his honor from day to
day," Burton-as-Becket tells the king, "he will serve you
faithfully." But later, alone, Becket wonders out loud, "What if
one day he should meet his honor in truth, face to face?" The
movie tells the story of how Becket meets his honor, the
honor of God. In the reading today, John urges us not to
improvise our honor but to keep God's word.

1 John 2:3–11
Psalm 96:1–2a,2b–3,5b–6
Luke 2:22–35

Friday

DECEMBER 30

• THE HOLY FAMILY OF JESUS, MARY, AND JOSEPH •

Put on love,
that is, the bond of perfection.
And let the peace of Christ control your hearts,
the peace into which you were also called in one body.
And be thankful.
—COLOSSIANS 3:14–15

A bond is an adhesive, a way of joining one thing securely, as in love, to another, but it's also a fetter. The next sentence has a similar tension. Peace is a form of freedom, freedom from anxiety, dissension, and war, and yet we are supposed to allow this freedom to control our hearts. Love and fetters. Freedom and control. But these paradoxes are the heart of our faith. We must lose our lives to save them. We must submit to love and peace. So during the craziness of this holiday season, with family obligations, visitors, heartbreak, and travel—enough to drive anyone mad—let yourself be fettered by love and controlled by peace.

Sirach 3:2–6,12–14 or
Colossians 3:12–21 or 3:12–17
Psalm 128:1–2,3,4–5
Matthew 2:13–15,19–23

What came to be through him was life.
—JOHN 1:3–4

The poet Edwin Muir once imagined Adam's dream of human
history, his vision of all that was to come. Adam sees the
generations of men and women running on a plain, identical
or interchangeable, growing in number and falling, rising,
separating, and clashing, mounds of bodies piling up. Adam
moves in closer and sees that these are not faceless masses
but that "each face was like his face." He wants to hail them
as sons of God but then remembers everything, "Eden, the
Fall, the Promise, and his place." He takes up the hands of all
his children and turns "in love and grief in Eve's encircling
arms." It is into this grand tragedy of human existence, each
single life as cherished and doomed as Adam's, that the words
of John's Gospel break: "this life was the light of the human
race . . . and the darkness has not overcome it."

1 John 2:18–21
Psalm 96:1–2,11–12,13
John 1:1–18

JANUARY 1

• SOLEMNITY OF MARY, THE HOLY MOTHER OF GOD •

When the fullness of time had come, God sent his Son,
born of a woman.
—GALATIANS 4:4

The "fullness of time" refers to all the time people spent
waiting for a Messiah, and also Mary's nine months of
pregnancy, and even more, the fullness of *all* time that pivots
on this moment. And what happened when the fullness of all
that time had come? God sent his son, born of a woman. It
makes all the difference that he didn't come into our world
like Zeus or Odin or Krishna; instead he was born as we are,
and he wasn't just born of a woman but of a particular
woman. She gave him flesh. It's for that reason that we pray,
over and over, "Hail Mary, Mother of God."

Numbers 6:22–27
Psalm 67:2–3,5,6,8 (2a)
Galatians 4:4–7
Luke 2:16–21

This happened in Bethany across the Jordan,
where John was baptizing.
—JOHN 1:28

One night a friend of mine, a devout Christian, was reading
some theology before bed. A particular argument in the book
struck her, and she said to her husband, "Maybe it all really
happened." He looked back, puzzled. "I thought we'd been
working off that assumption," he said. But I understand her
statement completely. Yes, we believe. That's been
established. But then we just go along, forgetting why, losing
touch with prayer, letting our reasons grow dim. That's why I
love the historical bits in the Gospels. It can all seem like
legend, full of symbolism and wisdom, the perennial wise
man crying out in the desert, who never really lived. But then
comes a moment like the one my friend had: it
happened—yes, it all really happened—in Bethany across
the Jordan, where John was baptizing.

1 John 2:22–28
Psalm 98:1,2–3ab,3cd–4
John 1:19–28

JANUARY 3

• THE MOST HOLY NAME OF JESUS •

Behold, the Lamb of God, who takes away
the sin of the world.
—JOHN 1:29

Do you remember the reading from yesterday? John the Baptist, really there, in Bethany. And into this real moment in time steps Jesus. John sees "the Spirit come down like a dove from the sky and remain upon him," and announces to the scattered penitents there, "Behold, the Lamb of God, who takes away the sin of the world." Thomas Merton once said he couldn't believe there was a time in his life when he didn't know what was happening in churches. I imagine this is what he meant: The priest, a real man at a given moment in time, holds up the body. "Behold the Lamb of God," he says to a scattered group of penitents. "Behold him who takes away the sin of the world." And then it happens, really happens, again.

1 John 2:29–3:6
Psalm 98:1,3cd–4,5–6
John 1:29–34

JANUARY 4

• ST. ELIZABETH ANN SETON, RELIGIOUS •

Let the rivers clap their hands,
the mountains shout with them for joy before the LORD.
—PSALM 98:8

My husband hates movies with talking animals. He used to
jump for the phone when the Nielsen Ratings guy called so
he could make a plea for fewer talking animals. He's softened
his take now that his daughter has half a hundred stuffed
animals, all with names, who apparently talk all the time. I
think he was on to something, though. When I hear that
rocks will sing or rivers clap their hands, I don't imagine
they'll appear with tiny mouths and hands like so many
screaming Muppets and act like we do. I imagine instead that
even those who have kept their peace will sing, not a song
like ours in its sounds, for theirs will be stony or watery or
full of bark, but like ours in its joy.

1 John 3:7–10
Psalm 98:1,7–8,9
John 1:35–42

Serve the LORD with gladness . . .
he made us . . .
his people, the flock he tends.
—PSALM 100:2–3

The other day I was listening to John Prine's song "Angel from Montgomery." In it, the singer Bonnie Raitt practically screams out the futility of life, the years rolling on by, going to work in the morning, coming home in the evening, and having nothing to say. Today is the feast day of John Neumann, bishop, tender of flocks. I'm sure every day people told him of this same fear that life is meaningless. But he responds: "Everyone who breathes . . . has a mission, has a work. We are not sent into this world for nothing; we are not born at random; we are not here, that we may go to bed at night, and get up in the morning . . . rear a family and die." He ends by urging and consoling us, just as the psalm does today, to rejoice in our work.

1 John 3:11–21
Psalm 100:1b–2,3,4,5
John 1:43–51

On coming up out of the water he saw
the heavens being torn open
and the Spirit, like a dove, descending upon him.
—MARK 1:10

In the readings three days ago, John saw the Spirit come
down. It is easy to picture Jesus standing there already
knowing everything. But today we see a different picture.
Jesus looked up like everyone else. Was he shocked to see
the sky being torn open and the Spirit descending? It's like a
dove, he might have thought, wondering where it would
alight. But then it came down upon him and a voice said:
"You are my beloved Son." Maybe this explains in part what
happened next. Jesus walked out into the desert for forty
days and nights. Might he have been coming to terms with
this vision of the Trinity, Father and Son and Holy Spirit, of
which he suddenly and incredibly found himself a part?

1 John 5:5–13
Psalm 147:12–13,14–15,19–20
Mark 1:7–11 or Luke 3:23–38 or
3:23,31–34,36,38

When the wine ran short,
the mother of Jesus said to him,
"They have no wine."
And Jesus said to her,
"Woman, how does your concern affect me?
My hour has not yet come."
—JOHN 2:3

Whenever Jesus speaks of "his hour" he means his passion. So his response, anything but a grumpy retort, asks Mary gently, "Are you ready for it all to begin?" And he calls her "woman," a title he will use again when he is looking down from the cross. With this first miracle, she will no longer be the mother of a particular son, with all its hidden intimacy; she will become the mother of everyone. There must have been a pause. She must have looked back across the table to see him as he was when he was just hers. God didn't foist himself upon humanity; he asked gently, twice—first through Gabriel and here again at Cana. And both times Mary said yes.

1 John 5:14–21
Psalm 149:1–2,3–4,5 and 6a and 9b
John 2:1–11

Sunday

JANUARY 8

• THE EPIPHANY OF THE LORD •

They were overjoyed at seeing the star,
and on entering the house
they saw the child with Mary his mother.
—MATTHEW 2:10–11

The three wise men were overjoyed at seeing the star, and on entering the house they saw the child with Mary, his mother. Mary his mother inside the house, her eyes full of stars, looked at them and her child. The child who shone bright as a star looked back at them and at Mary his mother and at the little house. The house opened up to take them in, for if it could expand enough to hold the child and Mary his mother, surely it could hold anything that came, even a star. The star stayed above them and above the house and the child and Mary his mother, long enough that we, too, could find it.

Isaiah 60:1–6
Psalm 72:1–2,7–8,10–11,12–13
Ephesians 3:2–3a,5–6
Matthew 2:1–12

JANUARY 9

• THE BAPTISM OF THE LORD •

John tried to prevent him, saying,
"I need to be baptized by you,
and yet you are coming to me?"
—MATTHEW 3:14

Lately my six-year-old has been putting her hands lightly
against my cheeks and saying, "I wish you were my
daughter." It breaks my heart. I'm not sure if my heart breaks
for my own mother who once held my face like that or for
my little daughter who is growing so fast or for myself who
loves them both. But thinking about this helps me imagine
what John must have felt when the Lord stood before him
and asked to be baptized. He balked. "Allow it," Jesus said,
then knelt down, as vulnerable as a child. Even though John
baptized Jesus, I think he still received the greater blessing.
And that's how we feel before God, held between a parent
and a child, both of them blessing us at once.

Isaiah 42:1–4,6–7 or Acts 10:34–38
Psalm 29:1–2,3–4,3,9–10 (11b)
Matthew 3:13–17

JANUARY 1o

It was not to angels that God subjected the world to come.
—HEBREWS 2:5

The Messiah did not come in glory, like Michael or Gabriel, a shining warrior to deliver his people. Instead, he was made to live, "for a little while" it says in Hebrews, "lower than the angels." And thank God, for we still tarry here, beneath the angels, each of our lives only a little while, and now we have hope that what is low can be redeemed and what is brief can be made eternal.

Hebrews 2:5–12
Psalm 8:2ab and 5,6–7,8–9
Mark 1:21–28

JANUARY 11

Therefore, he had to become like his brothers and sisters in every way.
—HEBREWS 2:17

This passage from Hebrews goes on to explain that because Christ was tested by what he suffered, he is able to help those who are being tested. Yes, but how does this help come? Here is St. Teresa of Ávila's beautiful take: "Christ has no body now but yours. No hands, no feet on earth but yours. Yours are the eyes through which he looks compassion on this world. Yours are the feet with which he walks to do good. Yours are the hands through which he blesses all the world. Yours are the hands, yours are the feet, yours are the eyes, you are his body. Christ has no body now on earth but yours." Christ became like us in every way, so that we could become like Christ.

Hebrews 2:14–18
Psalm 105:1–2,3–4,6–7,8–9
Mark 1:29–39

JANUARY 12

We have become partners of Christ, if only we hold the beginning of the reality firm until the end.
—HEBREWS 3:14

It is Ordinary Time in the liturgical calendar, and so we are back to the practices of the everyday. We wake up in the morning, go to sleep at night, raise our families. It would be easy to fall back into this routine and gradually despair. How often do I feel like that? Right now, in fact. I'm just trying to keep our days on track. But each of us was once like a knight, kneeling before the Lord. *Hold the beginning of the reality firm,* came a voice, *until the end.* We rode away full of furious and joyful intent. And then the days rolled on by, and gradually we forgot. But we are partners of Christ. The reality is just beginning. So hold it firm—your given plot of ground—until the end.

Hebrews 3:7–14
Psalm 95:6–7c,8–9,10–11
Mark 1:40–45

Jesus immediately knew in his mind what they were thinking to themselves, so he said, "Why are you thinking such things in your hearts?"
—MARK 2:8

I used to recoil at the idea of a God who knew my thoughts. I'm an introvert. I like to be alone. When I was a little girl I used to sit in the branches of a willow tree at night and imagine God spread out against the dark. And I preferred that distant, vast image to the one I later understood—God coming like an elder to notice and correct. But there is a third way, the God St. Teresa imagined dwelling in the innermost chamber of our souls, within which we also live and move and have our being. With this in mind I look back and see that girl in the tree more like a wick, flaming in the branches, sharing in the life of the very God who shimmered in the sky.

Hebrews 4:1–5,11
Psalm 78:3 and 4bc,6c–7,8
Mark 2:1–12

JANUARY 14

The word of God is living and effective, sharper than any two-edged sword, penetrating even between soul and spirit, joints and marrow.
—HEBREWS 4:12

Joints are hard pieces of bone. They define our shapes and form our gestures. Marrow is that soft tissue hidden inside of bone that renews our blood. Here, the analogy is that souls are like bones, spirits like marrow. Souls give our mortal lives shape; they are mind and body. Spirits are the hidden life force that share in the eternal life of God. According to Scripture, souls can die, just like bones. Think of that valley of dry bones Ezekiel once came upon. When the dry bones heard the word of God, they rattled together, bone-to-bone, growing skin and sinew. But only when God breathed his Spirit into them did they come to life, a vast army.

Hebrews 4:12–16
Psalm 19:8,9,10,15
Mark 2:13–17

JANUARY 15

• SECOND SUNDAY IN ORDINARY TIME •

Then said I, "Behold I come."
—PSALM 40:8

The refrain for this psalm is "Here I am, Lord; I come to do your will." I'm so used to singing these words in Mass that they usually flow by and I don't pay attention. But today it struck me as odd to say "Behold" to God, as if he were not all-seeing, or to say, "Here I am," as if I'd somehow managed to hide. In the Gospel, John the Baptist says, "Behold the Lamb of God," and this makes sense, for we are the distracted ones who must be told to look. So when we say, "Here I am," our words are not meant for God—he always knows where we are—but for ourselves. We are reminding ourselves that we are here, standing before the Lord. "Behold I come," we should whisper as we walk into Mass, or really any time at all.

Isaiah 49:3,5–6
Psalm 40:2,4,7–8,8–9,10 (8a,9a)
1 Corinthians 1:1–3
John 1:29–34

You are a priest forever according to the order of
Melchizedek.
—HEBREWS 5:6

Later in this passage Paul lists the characteristics of the new
Christian priesthood. The office is eternal, not fleeting.
These priests are appointed by God, not heredity. But the
most startling quality Paul cites is that a high priest "is able to
deal patiently with the ignorant and erring, for he himself is
beset by weakness." Not "acquainted with" but beset or
beleaguered by weakness. No wonder the priesthood is
losing numbers. But then Paul says that when Jesus was "in
the Flesh, he offered prayers and supplications with loud
cries and tears." A priest can bear his office, and we can bear
our lives, because Christ suffered all the inexpressible sorrow
and pain and guilt we've each experienced and cannot tell,
and he redeemed it all.

Hebrews 5:1–10
Psalm 110:1,2,3,4
Mark 2:18–22

Tuesday

JANUARY 17

• ST. ANTHONY, ABBOT •

*This we have as an anchor of the soul, sure and firm, which reaches into
the interior behind the veil.*
—HEBREWS 6:19

An anchor is a heavy object used to moor a boat to the
seabed. The related word *anchorite* means "one alone," a
hermit. St. Anthony, whose feast day we celebrate, is
considered the father of monks and the original anchorite.
He walked out into the desert and lived on little food in total
isolation. He was one alone, anchored only to God. I have
always felt thankful that our church includes these radical,
ascetic examples. For at some point in all of our lives, if only
at the very end, we will be called to give up everything and
walk alone, and then it will be only that anchor, heaved not
into the sea but into the heavens, that will help us finally
reach the interior behind the veil.

Hebrews 6:10–20
Psalm 111:1–2,4–5,9 and 10c
Mark 2:23–28

⇒ 52 ⇐

JANUARY 18

Is it lawful to do good on the sabbath rather than to do evil, to save life rather than to destroy it?
—MARK 3:4

Jesus is continuing an argument that began earlier. He is healing on the Sabbath and scandalizing the Pharisees. "The Sabbath was made for man, not man for the Sabbath," Jesus reminds them. But these days I think it is the first part of that sentence we need even more: "The Sabbath was made for man." God gave us the Sabbath, and yet we don't keep it. How would it change our weeks if we gave over one entire day to peace, family, prayer, breathing, rest? And even more, what might we find in that rest? In his book of Sabbath poems, Wendell Berry says that by resting on Sunday, we will be tended in ways we do not intend, carried forth and understood by what we cannot understand.

Hebrews 7:1–3,15–17
Psalm 110:1,2,3,4
Mark 3:1–6

JANUARY 19

They worship in a copy and shadow of the heavenly sanctuary.
—HEBREWS 8:5

Paul says that Jewish tabernacles were made rightly
according to the pattern shown on the mountains. But still
they were replicas. Before I read this, I might have said that
that's exactly what our churches are too, copies and shadows,
for don't we see darkly now, the world only a sketch of what
is to come? But lodged at the heart of every church is a
tabernacle holding the body of Christ. It's the real presence,
not a symbol or a clone, that makes our bricks and marble
and wood an outpost of heaven. And yet that is such a
radical notion that more often than not we choose to forget,
and we sit there before the very gates of heaven as if they
were shadows and let our thoughts drift away.

Hebrews 7:25–8:6
Psalm 40:7–8a,8b–9,10,17
Mark 3:7–12

I will put my laws in their minds
and I will write them upon their hearts.
—HEBREWS 8:10

The entire letter to the Hebrews is a discussion of the
transition from the old covenant to the new. "The real
novelty of the New Testament," wrote Pope Benedict, "lies
not so much in new ideas as in the figure of Christ himself,
who gives flesh and blood to those concepts—an
unprecedented realism." We see that same movement, from
idea to reality, here. The law was once a set of ideas written
in stone, somehow external to us, but now it lives in our
hearts. This transition from old to new, from idea to reality,
isn't just a historical progression but takes place in the course
of all our lives. We must perpetually learn that what is true is
really true, as real and near as our beating hearts, and we
cannot hide.

Hebrews 8:6–13
Psalm 85:8 and 10,11–12,13–14
Mark 3:13–19

JANUARY 21

• ST. AGNES, VIRGIN AND MARTYR •

He is out of his mind.
—MARK 3:21

My eight-year-old son is as self-conscious as I am, worrying
what the world thinks. His sister has adopted an almost
opposite stance. She wears wild costumes and screams from
the car top. She is still only six years old, her baby fat not
entirely gone, her eyes still shining their newness, so even as
we cringe we can't help laughing. And she helps us to come
out of ourselves, out of our minds. There is a medieval
tradition of holy or blessed fools, saints who openly acted
mad—throwing nuts, juggling, screaming in the streets—but
who secretly healed and prayed and wept. We aren't all
called to act crazy, but it might help if we practiced
sometimes, for Christ does call us to come out of our minds
and be like him.

Hebrews 9:2–3,11–14
Psalm 47:2–3,6–7,8–9
Mark 3:20–21

Sunday

JANUARY 22

• THIRD SUNDAY IN ORDINARY TIME •

Anguish has taken wing, dispelled is darkness:
for there is no gloom where but now there was distress.
—ISAIAH 8:23

Meltem Aktaş, an artist in my parish, once painted a beautiful portrait of despair. In the painting, a woman stands with a look of distress on her face, her arms curved about her, one over her head, the other under her rib cage, as if cradling herself. Above her flies a broken skeleton of a bird, anguish taking wing, and gloom seems to move about them in blurry clouds. And yet if you look more closely, the lines of the bird's body and its spread wings form a cross. So the painting can also be seen as an image of the Crucifixion, which looked like anguish until, behold, the darkness cleared away.

Isaiah 8:23–9:3
Psalm 27:1,4,13–14 (1a)
1 Corinthians 1:10–13,17
Matthew 4:12–23 or 4:12–17

JANUARY 23

• DAY OF PRAYER FOR THE LEGAL PROTECTION OF UNBORN CHILDREN •

*If that were so, he would have had to suffer repeatedly from the
foundation of the world.*
—HEBREWS 9:26

In this passage the writer is saying that if the Crucifixion
were nothing more than the sacrifice of animals, then that
killing would have to be done again and again. Instead, he
says, "But now once for all he has appeared at the end of the
ages." Milan Kundera, in his novel *The Unbearable Lightness of
Being*, discusses the idea of eternal return: the appalling myth
that everything that happens, whether joy or torture,
happens over and over ad infinitum. In contrast, our lives,
which only happen once, are so light they can sometimes
seem only half real. Which do we prefer, he asks, lightness or
weight? But in some real sense we don't have to choose. We
believe the Crucifixion stands both in and outside time,
happening once but never lost, and so tethers our fleeting
lives to eternity.

Hebrews 9:15,24–28
Psalm 98:1,2–3ab,3cd–4,5–6
Mark 3:22–30

⇒ 58 ⇐

Tuesday

JANUARY 24

• ST. FRANCIS DE SALES, BISHOP AND DOCTOR OF THE CHURCH •

I have waited, waited for the LORD,
and he stooped toward me.
—PSALM 40:2

Today is the feast day of St. Francis de Sales, but I'm thinking instead of another saint, Vincent de Paul. The psalm today reminds me of another painting by artist Meltem Aktaş. St. Vincent is shown handing a piece of bread to a beggar. Somehow you can tell from the painting—maybe it's the light that infuses both sky and ground—that the tattered beggar is Jesus. But it's not quite clear who is giving and who is receiving. We wait and wait for the Lord, and then there he is, stooping toward us. And "it is only for your love alone," says St. Vincent himself, "that the poor will forgive you the bread you give them."

Hebrews 10:1–10
Psalm 40:2 and 4ab,7–8a,10,11
Mark 3:31–35

⇒ 59 ⇐

JANUARY 25

*On that journey as I drew near to Damascus, about noon a great light
from the sky suddenly shone around me.*
—ACTS 22:6

Paul's companions saw a great light but heard no voice.
Earlier in Acts, it says that they heard a voice but saw
nothing. My father, once an atheist, used to present this
conflicting testimony to any evangelist who had the
misfortune to knock on our door. Like Paul, my father makes
arguments for a living. Paul was a lawyer, my father a
mathematician. But with age my father has come to see
arguments differently. It isn't the argument itself that holds
truth but something that lies beyond. So often inspiration
has come to my father in a sudden burst, and only later will
he work out a proof. Other mathematicians have reported a
voice coming in their dreams. Today my father is Catholic
and despairs of the young man he once was who knew so
little of Truth.

Acts 22:3–16 or 9:1–22
Psalm 117:1bc,2
Mark 16:15–18

Take care what you hear. The measure with which you measure will be measured out to you.
—MARK 4:24

Jesus cautions us not to gossip and judge, to take care how we measure out our assessments of others. I see myself with rulers and scales, stingy and covetous, carefully measuring myself against the world. But in a similar passage in Luke, the focus shifts from judging to giving: "Give and gifts will be given you; a good measure, packed together, shaken down and overflowing, will be poured into your lap." The image that comes to mind for me is of flour, packed down in its cup, packed down until no more will fit in, but still poured out until overflowing. And Jesus means for this abundance not to be dry goods but our very lives. He is telling us not to measure at all, for a good measure, unlike a ruler or cup, has no markings.

2 Timothy 1:1–8 or Titus 1:1–5
Psalm 96:1–2a,2b–3,7–8a,10
Mark 4:21–25

This is how it is with the Kingdom of God; it is as if a man were to scatter seed on the land and would sleep and rise night and day and the seed would sprout and grow, he knows not how.
—MARK 4:26–27

At one point in Arnold Lobel's children's book *Frog and Toad Together*, Toad decides to plant a garden. He scatters seeds on the land. Nothing happens. He yells at the seeds to start growing. Nothing happens. He reads stories to the seeds. He plays music. Nothing happens. Finally, Lobel writes, "Toad felt very tired and he fell asleep." When he woke, "little green plants were coming out of the ground." This is how it is with the kingdom of God. So go about your good work, sleep and rise as you always do, and have faith that God will bring your actions, no matter how, to fruition.

Hebrews 10:32–39
Psalm 37:3–4,5–6,23–24,39–40
Mark 4:26–34

Saturday

JANUARY 28

• ST. THOMAS AQUINAS, PRIEST AND DOCTOR OF THE CHURCH •

Who then is this whom even wind and sea obey?
—MARK 4:41

"Not being able to do the work of angels in choir," said St. Thomas Aquinas, "we can at least write about them." And write he did, furiously, day and night. But then on December 6 in the year 1273, his writing, like the sudden quelling of a storm, abruptly came to a halt. His brother, Reginald, begged for an explanation, and St. Thomas said, "All that I have written seems like straw after the things that have been revealed to me." It was as if he had seen the wind and sea obey a command. I've never had a vision that changed my life, but knowing that that great man of reason fell to his knees before the real thing is almost as good.

Hebrews 11:1–2,8–19
Luke 1:69–70,71–72,73–75
Mark 4:35–41

JANUARY 29

• FOURTH SUNDAY IN ORDINARY TIME •

God chose the lowly and despised of the world, those who count for
nothing, to reduce to nothing those who are something.
—1 CORINTHIANS 1:28

In the movie *Amadeus*, about Mozart's life, his contemporary
Salieri is driven mad by his failure to live up to Mozart's
greatness. In the end Salieri dubs himself the "Patron Saint of
Mediocrity" and is shown being pushed down the hallway of
an asylum calling out grandly to his fellow patients,
"Mediocrity is everywhere. I absolve you." It's supposed to be
amusing, but it also sums up one of our greatest fears: that in
the end we'll count for nothing. Yet God tells us today that
it's not mediocrity we need to be absolved of but pride,
considering ourselves wise or strong or important when God
cares for none of these things. In God's eyes we are naked,
unadorned by achievement and status and good looks, and
he loves us for ourselves.

Zephaniah 2:3; 3:12–13
Psalm 146:6–7,8–9,9–10
1 Corinthians 1:26–31
Matthew 5:1–12a

JANUARY 30

Yet all these, though approved because of their faith, did not receive what had been promised.
—HEBREWS 11:39

Paul gives a long catalog of Old Testament acts of martyrdom. "They were stoned, sawed in two, put to death at sword's point," he tells us. And then later, "They wandered about in deserts and on mountains, in caves and in crevices of the earth." Yet they did not receive what had been promised. Why not? Because God had foreseen something better, Paul says, and here is the part I love: "so that without us they should not be made perfect." It is a startling idea. They died, and yet their lives were not finished. Those who came before live in us, not as fading memories but in some real way, and we will live on in those who come much later. By living we help fulfill the lives of others.

Hebrews 11:32–40
Psalm 31:20,21,22,23,24
Mark 5:1–20

Tuesday

JANUARY 31

• ST. JOHN BOSCO, PRIEST •

He took the child by the hand and said to her, "Talitha koum," which
means, "Little girl, I say to you, arise!"
—MARK 5:41

When my baby died, it was this story I played over and over
in my head. My mind jerked a thousand times a day between
the hope of *talitha koum* and the reality of death. It is death,
not life, that seems unnatural; we've just been trained by the
mortality around us to accept death. But when God acts, as
the psalm will tell us tomorrow, his kindness is from eternity
to eternity. So the whispered *talitha koum* echoes through
time to all of us. And I hope it will be like that, not a rising
up of angels, unrecognizable and austere, but as if each of our
loved ones merely sat up in bed, just as they were, and we
had the glorious chance to give them something to eat.

Hebrews 12:1–4
Psalm 22:26b–27,28 and 30,31–32
Mark 5:21–43

FEBRUARY 1

*So strengthen your drooping hands and your weak knees. Make straight
paths for your feet, that what is lame may not be dislocated but healed.*
—HEBREWS 12:12–13

There is an episode from Natalie Goldberg's book, *Writing
Down the Bones*, that I've always remembered. One day, feeling
hopeless, Goldberg goes to her Zen teacher for advice, and
he says simply, "When in doubt, take positive action for the
good." In his wisdom he realized that she didn't need gentle
words or analysis, at least not at that moment, but a simple
path for her feet. Paul takes the same approach today. When
all else seems impossible, when you are full of doubt, get up!
Strengthen your drooping hands and weak knees! You don't
have to do it all right now; just put one foot in front of the
other. Take positive action for the good.

Hebrews 12:4–7,11–15
Psalm 103:1–2,13–14,17–18a
Mark 6:1–6

Thursday

FEBRUARY 2

• THE PRESENTATION OF THE LORD •

Lift up, O gates, your lintels;
reach up, you ancient portals,
that the king of glory may come in!
—PSALM 24:7

The Presentation of the Lord, celebrating the presentation of
Jesus at the temple, is another day, like Christmas, like
Epiphany, when we meet Christ as if for the first time. It is
also beautifully called Candlemas, and it marks the midpoint
between Christmas and Easter. The pure candle wax, "drawn
out by mother bees," as it says in the Easter Exsultet,
represents the flesh Mary gave her son. The wick of each
candle is the light of Christ, "divided yet never dimmed." So
bring your tapers to Mass, walk up to the altar and imagine
those ancient gates lifting up their heads like two great lions.
Lift your head up with them and meet Christ once again.
And then through the dark of winter, let your candles burn.

Malachi 3:1–4
Psalm 24:7,8,9,10
Hebrews 2:14–18
Luke 2:22–40 or 2:22–32

Friday

FEBRUARY 3

• ST. BLAISE, BISHOP AND MARTYR • ST. ANSGAR, BISHOP •

*Do not neglect hospitality, for through it some have unknowingly
entertained angels.*
—HEBREWS 13:2

If you were certain that one day a real angel would come
disguised to your door and dine with you, would you not ask
everyone in? Would you not keep a place set just in case?
And study each visitor's face to see if he or she might be the
one? And after a time might you not begin to see each one as
God does? And begin to take pity on their wrinkles or youth,
feel tenderly toward their clothes and hair, and observe the
way they laugh to disguise their sorrow? And then might you
no longer notice or care whether angels sat at your table
or not?

Hebrews 13:1–8
Psalm 27:1,3,5,8b–9abc
Mark 6:14–29

FEBRUARY 4

May the God of peace, who brought up from the dead, the great shepherd
of the sheep . . . furnish you with all that is good.
—HEBREWS 13:20–21

Usually it is the Good Shepherd who rescues us. He calls
each of his sheep by name. He gathers us back into the fold.
He goes in search of even a single one who is lost and
furnishes us with all that is good. But today it is the Good
Shepherd who needs to be rescued. Paul tells us that God
brought the Good Shepherd up from the dead. And it is by
this act alone that the Shepherd is able to rescue us. It's the
mystery of our faith, that Jesus died and rose. We sing it on
our knees at every Mass. For if this didn't happen, we'd have
no God of peace, nor any Good Shepherd.

Hebrews 13:15–17,20–21
Psalm 23:1–3a,3b–4,5,6
Mark 6:30–34

He shall never be moved;
the just one shall be in everlasting remembrance.
—PSALM 112:6

This psalm probably means that the just man is remembered
forever, but I love the inverse idea of a person being in a state
of everlasting remembrance. To remember is to be mindful,
to gather one's thoughts within. The word *remember* is often
used as a synonym for *recollect*, which similarly means to
recover or collect oneself after a distraction. St. Teresa of
Ávila talks about the fatigue that arises when we try to
overcome our disperse minds, which are tending always
toward exterior things. But if we can manage it, she says, we
will shut ourselves up "within this little heaven of the soul,
where dwells the Maker of heaven and earth." Yes, and where
dwells the one who never forgets.

Isaiah 58:7–10
Psalm 112:4–5,6–7,8–9 (4a)
1 Corinthians 2:1–5
Matthew 5:13–16

*In the beginning, when God created the heavens and the earth, the earth
was a formless wasteland, and darkness covered the abyss, while a
mighty wind swept over the waters.*
—GENESIS 1:1–2

In today's scientific world, it's hard to imagine God's presence
stretching back through time into prehistory. We picture
only vast jungles and seas teeming with evolving life-forms,
everything unconscious. That is one reason I love Terrence
Malick's movie *The Tree of Life*. He creates a visceral sense that
God has always been here. At one point we hear the prayer
of a heartbroken mother whispered over prehistoric waters.
There are no people yet, no one to make sense of language,
so we know that for this voice to sound at all, God is
listening. Genesis recounts the beginning of time. But God
was there already, before the sun and moon, hearing all our
desperate prayers.

Genesis 1:1–19
Psalm 104:1–2a,5–6,10 and 12,24 and 35c
Mark 6:53–56

FEBRUARY 7

God said, "Let us make man in our image, after our likeness."
—GENESIS 1:26

In his writings on Genesis, St. Ambrose reflects on this passage, cataloging all the ways our physical selves are not made in God's image. Our eyes see as God sees, but they don't see much, not even what is behind us. Our ears hear as God hears, but they can't hear through walls or across far distances. But our souls are free to wander far and wide. So it is through the mind, Ambrose says, which "beholds the absent and embraces in its vision countries beyond the horizon," that we are made in God's image. But we are not God, we are *after his likeness*, a reflection. So we must take care in which direction our wandering souls point.

Genesis 1:20–2:4a
Psalm 8:4–5,6–7,8–9
Mark 7:1–13

FEBRUARY 8

• ST. JEROME EMILIANI, PRIEST • ST. JOSEPHINE BAKHITA, VIRGIN •

The LORD God formed man out of the clay of the ground and blew into his nostrils the breath of life, and so man became a living being.
—GENESIS 2:7

I live in my head, thinking, writing, walking about in a daze, forgetting my life. That is why I love my memories of giving birth. I was wholly in my body. And later, when my baby lay there breathing on my chest, her soul seeming to float inchoate around her, not yet tacked down by life, it was her tiny toes and eyelashes I adored. The Lord God formed us out of clay. I imagine this now as the long millennia of evolution, a slow fashioning from stardust to carbon to bone. And then God's breath made us live. But when Adam finally lay there breathing, fresh and real, I bet God cherished his body at least as much as his soul.

Genesis 2:4b–9,15–17
Psalm 104:1–2a,27–28,29bc–30
Mark 7:14–23

FEBRUARY 9

*This one, at last, is bone of my bones
and flesh of my flesh.*
—GENESIS 2:23

I like to imagine Adam on the long morning of the sixth day
walking about awestruck, seeing only how the world looked
through his eyes. It was out of pity for his poor sight that
God broke Adam's rib, rolled and burnished it between his
palms and whispered Adam awake into a peopled world. At
first Adam could see only how the feet of his rib moved in
the dirt and how the hands of his rib looked beautiful peeling
a fruit. How long was it before he looked up and saw not his
rib but a separate being, alone in herself? *Alone, like I am also
alone*, he must have thought, and then been able to picture
her even when he closed his eyes. Ever since, we have longed
for communion.

Genesis 2:18–25
Psalm 128:1–2,3,4–5
Mark 7:24–30

FEBRUARY 10

• ST. SCHOLASTICA, VIRGIN •

When they heard the sound of the LORD God moving about in the garden at the breezy time of the day, the man and his wife hid themselves from the LORD God among the trees of the garden.
—GENESIS 3:8

What was it like? I imagine it came from all directions, the sound of God moving in the garden, at first mixed in with the breeze, but then something else, bigger, leaves being brushed aside, feet like a thousand feet, coming closer and closer. What would you do? Run to greet him or hide? In today's psalm we have a different image. "You are my shelter," David says, "with glad cries of freedom you will ring me round." In both cases, God closes in, surrounds, but how do we get from an experience of fear to freedom? We get there through love, which brought God so close he dwelt among us.

Genesis 3:1–8
Psalm 32:1–2,5,6,7
Mark 7:31–37

FEBRUARY 11

When he expelled the man, he settled him east of the garden of Eden; and he stationed the cherubim and the fiery revolving sword, to guard the way to the tree of life.
—GENESIS 3:23–24

At first it sounds terrible, this place of banishment. We imagine some distant, apocalyptic land. But then we remember that east of Eden is here, the world we know. E. B. White once said, "All that I hope to say in books, all that I ever hope to say, is that I love the world." We love it so much we never want to leave, but we have to. It's as if we live both in and outside the garden at once, always aware that at some point we'll be banished. So we spend our lives making our way to the cross, the tree of life, which will allow us to stay.

Genesis 3:9–24
Psalm 90:2,3–4abc,5–6,12–13
Mark 8:1–10

He has set before you fire and water
to whichever you choose, stretch forth your hand.
—SIRACH 15:16

This passage from Sirach describes something like a game of wits. Two chalices are set on the table, one with poison, the other without, and you have to figure out which one is which. Fire keeps you warm and fends off danger, but water is essential to life. The choice is clear. But in the end I'm not sure it really matters, for God tells us that whether we walk through water or fire, he shall be with us. The real choice is what Sirach says next: "Before man are life and death, good and evil, whichever he chooses shall be given him." But our conception of life is different from God's. We try to stay afloat, away from the flames, when really he wants us to follow him, even when it seems we might drown or burn.

Sirach 15:15–20
Psalm 119:1–2,4–5,17–18,33–34 (1b)
1 Corinthians 2:6–10
Matthew 5:17–37 or
5:20–22a,27–28,33–34a,37

FEBRUARY 13

Then the LORD asked Cain, "Where is your brother Abel?"
He answered, "I do not know. Am I my brother's keeper?"
—GENESIS 4:9

Earlier in this passage it says, "Abel became a keeper of flocks." *Keep* once meant "to hold" and then "to watch" or "to observe." Now it means something more like preserving, or causing to continue on. But the problem is that the things we try to preserve are fleeting. Cain killed his brother, but even if he hadn't, Abel still would have died someday. Doesn't the soil cry out for all the dead? There is no doubt that we've been made keepers of many things. But the answer to how to keep or hold or preserve that which we know to be passing is not a simple matter. What in your life has been laid to your charge? What does it mean for you to keep it?

Genesis 4:1–15,25
Psalm 50:1 and 8,16bc–17,20–21
Mark 8:11–13

Tuesday

FEBRUARY 14

• SS. CYRIL, MONK, AND METHODIUS, BISHOP •

*So the LORD said: "I will wipe out from the earth the men whom I
have created."*
—GENESIS 6:7

Today the readings tell us of God's anger. In Genesis, God
regrets that he made man on the earth. In the psalm, God's
voice thunders over the vast waters. In the Gospel Jesus says
over and over, "Do you not understand?" We are used to
thinking of anger as erupting out of sin, out of our
short-tempered, self-centered ways, but here God in his
perfection is furious. He does it for us. For we are like
children and need to see, sometimes in dramatic ways, the
effect of our actions. If God's anger had been like ours, it
would have wiped everything out for good. Yet God made an
ark. And some say the ark is really his church. It still carries
us today.

Genesis 6:5–8; 7:1–5,10
Psalm 29:1a and 2,3ac–4,3b and 9c–10
Mark 8:14–21

Putting spittle on his eyes he laid his hands on the man and asked, "Do you see anything?"
Looking up the man replied, "I see people looking like trees and walking."
—MARK 8:23–24

Usually when Jesus healed it was instantaneous—a brush of his cloak, a touch of his hand. But here he allows the man to have a more gradual experience of redemption. To me that middle vision, no longer blind but not quite seeing yet, seems like purgatory. We will be there looking glory in the face, and yet everything will seem off kilter. It will take time for our vision to clear. Or maybe that middle vision was prophetic. Maybe the blind man saw a person in the shape of a tree, nailed there, who, incredibly, rose and walked.

Genesis 8:6–13,20–22
Psalm 116:12–13,14–15,18–19
Mark 8:22–26

FEBRUARY 16

Dread fear of you shall come upon all the animals of the earth.
—GENESIS 9:2

Ever since Eden, the world has been breaking apart. Once
man had gentle dominion over the beasts; they came when
he called. Now God says, "Into your power they are
delivered. Every creature that is alive shall be yours to eat."
And so we are estranged. The writer J. R. R. Tolkien called
our desire to have communion with other living things one
of our primordial desires. I see it in my daughter, how she
longs to touch, to tame, even to embody animals. And
sometimes I look at our dog and have a sudden rush of
gratitude. He's come over from the outside, overcome the
dread fear, and, like a brave little saint, pads about my house
in peace, lays his head on my lap, lets me pat his belly, and
gives me hope that a greater communion is possible.

Genesis 9:1–13
Psalm 102:16–18,19–21,29 and 22–23
Mark 8:27–33

Friday

FEBRUARY 17

• THE SEVEN HOLY FOUNDERS OF SERVITE ORDER •

What profit is there for one to gain the whole world and forfeit his life?
—MARK 8:36

We understand in the context that when he says "life," Jesus means eternal life. Some other translations use the word *soul*. These days we are used to thinking of our bodies as precious. We exercise, we buy organic, we worry about pollution. But our souls? "The soul is a terrible reality," says Oscar Wilde's character Dorian Gray. "It can be bought and sold and bartered away. It can be poisoned or made perfect. There is a soul in each one of us. I know it." We must take care, for like the body, the soul can be poisoned or made perfect; it can be lost or gained. And there is a soul in each one of us.

Genesis 11:1–9
Psalm 33:10–11,12–13,14–15
Mark 8:34–9:1

�⋋

FEBRUARY 18

*Faith is the realization of what is hoped for and evidence of things
not seen.*
—HEBREWS 11:1

St. Augustine wrote that when you hope, you do not yet
have what you are hoping for, but that hope gives way to
faith, and faith to the real thing. I once told a friend that I'd
never had an experience of God's presence, only the desire
for it. And he said, "But don't you realize that is God?" God's
presence begins in us as the feeling of something missing. "I
mean," Augustine continued, "you do not have your hands on
anything when you have them on faith." We know God is
there not because we experience his fullness but because we
hold an emptiness that has not yet been filled.

Hebrews 11:1–7
Psalm 145:2–3,4–5,10–11
Mark 9:2–13

FEBRUARY 19

• SEVENTH SUNDAY IN ORDINARY TIME •

Take no revenge and cherish no grudge against any of your people.
—LEVITICUS 19:18

My Indian friend's grandmother, whom they called Beegie, always stood at the stove perpetually preparing food. We'd sit in the kitchen talking while Beegie cooked. Even though she watched American soap operas every day, she didn't speak any English. During one of these kitchen talks, someone mentioned so-and-so who was having an affair, and Beegie spun around. "Affair?" she said, tilting her head. We all laughed at this one word she'd picked out. She was probably just happy to finally participate, but I'm certainly like that, pricking up my ears at scandal or any time a grudge is mentioned. It's a quick way to get a good story. And yet it comes at a cost, for what we spend our time discussing is what we come to cherish, even if it's just a petty grudge.

Leviticus 19:1–2,17–18
Psalm 103:1–2,3–4,8,10,12–13 (8a)
1 Corinthians 3:16–23
Matthew 5:38–48

FEBRUARY 20

Then the boy's father cried out, "I do believe, help my unbelief!"
—MARK 9:24

Once when my children were very young and I was
overwhelmed, I told a friend that I was struggling to believe.
I can still see us sitting on a blanket in the park behind my
house while our children wandered into the grass. She said,
"I've come to see my felt experience of faith as beside the
point." I took this to mean that having a visceral experience
of God is not really what faith is about, and her words helped
me. Doubt is an inevitable part of the life of faith. So instead
of worrying that your faith has vanished, let this be your
prayer: "I do believe; help my unbelief."

Sirach 1:1–10
Psalm 93:1ab,1cd–2,5
Mark 9:14–29

FEBRUARY 21

• ST. PETER DAMIAN, BISHOP AND DOCTOR OF THE CHURCH •

If anyone wishes to be first, he shall be the last of all.
—MARK 9:35

Yesterday I watched my children race up a hill to be king of the mountain. I remember how my feet also used to pound across the wet grass with single-minded purpose. Children want to see their wills at work, learn what their bodies can do, test the boundary between themselves and others. But later this desire to get there first must give way to the real challenge. Flannery O'Connor once wrote of one of her characters, "He understood that [agony] was all a man could carry into death to give his Maker and he burned with shame that he had so little of it to take with him." Her vision might be too grim, but it's not status or fortune that matters in the end, only what we ourselves, through love and sorrow, have become.

Sirach 2:1–11
Psalm 37:3–4,18–19,27–28,39–40
Mark 9:30–37

FEBRUARY 22

• THE CHAIR OF ST. PETER THE APOSTLE •

Do not lord it over those assigned to you, but be examples to the flock.
—1 PETER 5:3

Today is the only day of the year we celebrate a chair, in a celebration that dates all the way back to the fourth century. This chair, the Cathedra Petri, worm-eaten and slashed, is a rather small, carved, oaken armchair. It's actually no longer thought to be the original chair of Peter but a symbol of it. An empty chair indicates a missing person. It's a place at the table, a reserved seat, and it offers the hope of a continued, invisible presence. When I imagine Peter's original chair, I think of Peter himself, fiery and loyal, bumbling and honest, and I miss him, if it is possible to miss someone you've never met. And I imagine that future time when every chair at the feast will be filled, and no one will be missed anymore.

1 Peter 5:1–4
Psalm 23:1–3a,4,5,6
Matthew 16:13–19

FEBRUARY 23

• ST. POLYCARP, BISHOP AND MARTYR •

Everyone will be salted with fire.
—MARK 9:49

In the Talmud, it says that when God prays, he prays for his mercy to overcome his anger. But the readings today warn that if we focus too much on mercy, we might forget God's anger and think sin doesn't matter. Jesus tells us, "If your hand causes you to sin, cut it off." And your foot, he adds. And your eye. "Upon the wicked alights his wrath," says Sirach. We picture the Old Testament God raging, demanding severed bits of our bodies. But Sirach also says, "Mercy and anger are alike to him." However, we are the ones who range from mercy to anger, not God. So we must guard against sin but also trust that God's one prayer is only for our goodness. It's a prayer so bright and pure that it can feel like fire.

Sirach 5:1–8
Psalm 1:1–2,3,4 and 6
Mark 9:41–50

FEBRUARY 24

A faithful friend is a sturdy shelter.
—SIRACH 6:14

The twelfth-century Cistercian monk Aelred of Rievaulx wrote a small work that has become a classic, *Spiritual Friendship*. It would be easy to think that the word *spiritual* in the title refers to the quality of the friendship, spiritual friendships being the highest ones, something hard to attain. But Aelred is careful to say that what makes a friendship spiritual is not its lofty height so much as its origin and direction. Spiritual friendship, Aelred says, begins in God, continues in God, and is perfected in God. It's a road or a way, not a static condition. So when you imagine yourself as a sturdy shelter for a friend, or when you take shelter in the friendship of another, don't worry if your shelter is not yet perfect. You are building it as you go.

Sirach 6:5–17
Psalm 119:12,16,18,27,34,35
Mark 10:1–12

FEBRUARY 25

The wind sweeps over him and he is gone,
and his place knows him no more.
—PSALM 103:16

In her memoir *Out of Africa*, Isak Dinesen asks, "Does Africa
know a song of me? Will the air over the plain quiver with a
color that I have had on, or the children invent a game in
which my name is, or the full moon throw a shadow over the
gravel of the drive that was like me, or will the eagles of the
Ngong Hills look out for me?" We long for people and places
to recall us. We long for immortality. But the psalm today
tells us that wind will sweep us away and our places know us
no more. And yet it also says that in his compassion God
remembers we are dust. And hasn't he promised to someday
raise up this dust, this gravel and air, that holds our shadows?

Sirach 17:1–15
Psalm 103:13–14,15–16,17–18
Mark 10:13–16

FEBRUARY 26

Thus should one regard us: as servants of Christ and stewards of the mysteries of God.
—1 CORINTHIANS 4:1

Every year most churches have a stewardship campaign that urges parishioners to reassess what they are giving back to the church. The idea is that everything comes from God, and we are stewards or managers of these things. But today we are called stewards, not of time, talent, and treasure, but of the mysteries of God. I love the idea of being the manager of a mystery. It seems to bring the fleeting world of business right up against the eternal. But what could it mean to manage such things? "Now it is of course required of stewards," says Paul, "that they be found trustworthy." The mysteries of God are incredibly given over to our hands; we're not even sure what that means, but in this case in particular, we must be found trustworthy.

Isaiah 49:14–15
Psalm 62:2–3,6–7,8–9 (6a)
1 Corinthians 4:1–5
Matthew 6:24–34

It is easier for a camel to pass through the eye of a needle than for one who is rich to enter the Kingdom of God.
—MARK 10:25

The disciples are astonished and ask, "Then who can be saved?" And Jesus says, "For men it is impossible, but not for God. All things are possible for God." Before when I would read this passage, I couldn't get beyond the disciples' question, their fear that the way to immortality is impossibly narrow. But reading it with today's psalm, I hear only reassurance. The psalm calls us to confess our faults, cover not our guilt, and in turn God will keep the deep, overflowing waters from reaching us. It says that in times of distress, God is our shelter. So who can be saved? Everyone. Everyone, that is, who realizes that our strength alone is never enough.

Sirach 17:20–24
Psalm 32:1–2,5,6,7
Mark 10:17–27

FEBRUARY 28

To keep the law is a great oblation.
—SIRACH 35:1

An oblation is an offering, and an oblate one who becomes
the offering. Jesus is the ultimate oblate, the one who
showed us that God doesn't want burnt sacrifices—he wants
our lives. Kathleen Norris's book *The Cloister Walk* chronicles
her journey as a Benedictine oblate. Right before making the
decision to tie herself to the Benedictines, she says to a
monk, "I can't imagine why God of all people would want me
as an offering. But if God is foolish enough to take me as I
am, I guess I better do it." The monk replies, "You're ready."
Lent begins tomorrow, when we'll all be asked to make
offerings of our lives. And have no doubt about it, God is
foolish enough to take every one of us as we are.

Sirach 35:1–12
Psalm 50:5–6,7–8,14 and 23
Mark 10:28–31

Wednesday

MARCH 1

• ASH WEDNESDAY •

Even now, says the LORD,
return to me with your whole heart.
—JOEL 2:12

Today the readings are a call for us to come together. "Blow
the trumpet," says Joel. "Proclaim a fast, / call an assembly; /
Gather the people, / notify the congregation." I love to hear
the bells toll from my house and then encounter people
walking through the streets of our neighborhood, all heading
to Mass and later with ashes on their foreheads, walking
home. The poet Kathleen Norris writes, "Only Christ could
have brought us all together, in this place, doing such absurd
but necessary things." I imagine bells tolling in
neighborhoods, towns, cities around the world. "Behold,"
says St. Paul today, "now is a very acceptable time; behold,
now is the day of salvation." We are called together today,
this great human community; we are notified and gathered,
to rend our hearts and begin again.

Joel 2:12–18
Psalm 51:3–4,5–6ab,12–13,14 and 17
2 Corinthians 5:20–6:2
Matthew 6:1–6,16–18

I have set before you life and death, the blessing and the curse.
—DEUTERONOMY 30:19

Today's verse makes me think of two movie clips. In *The African Queen*, Katharine Hepburn primly condemns a drunk Humphrey Bogart. "Nature, Mr. Allnut," she scoffs, "is what we are put in this world to rise above." The movie *The Tree of Life* opens with a more somber take: "The nuns taught us there are two ways," comes a voice, "the way of nature and the way of grace. You have to choose which one you'll follow." In both films, the way of grace becomes synonymous with the way of love. "Choose life!" Moses urges us today. And we want to scream back, "Yes!" But our lives are such a mess, so cluttered with things and confusion and heartbreak, that we're not sure which way is which. Lent is a time to pause and figure out which path we're on.

Deuteronomy 30:15–20
Psalm 1:1–2,3,4 and 6
Luke 9:22–25

Friday

MARCH 3

Do you call this a fast,
a day acceptable to the LORD?
—ISAIAH 58:5

In a tone that is almost sarcastic, God says he wants no more heads bowing like reeds, no more sackcloth and ashes. He wants a deeper, more sincere fast, which he sums up as "clothing the naked when you see them, / and not turning your back on your own." These are tasks close at hand. The word *fast* means simply "to hold firm." So God is telling us we must bring the same determination that allows us to abstain from food to the deeper tasks in our lives. Don't fast "to make your voice heard on high," God tells us. Instead, look for a more pressing task, one that is your own, to hold firm. If you find it, God says, "then your light shall break forth like the dawn."

Isaiah 58:1–9a
Psalm 51:3–4,5–6ab,18–19
Matthew 9:14–15

Saturday

MARCH 4

• SATURDAY AFTER ASH WEDNESDAY * ST. CASIMIR •

Keep my life, for I am devoted to you.
—PSALM 86:2

On the first day of Advent, more than three months ago, we heaved our souls into the mountain and asked God to keep them. Later, we thought about the difficulty of being keepers of anything, since everything is passing away. Shortly before Pope John Paul II died, he wrote, "And yet, I do not altogether die. What is indestructible in me remains! What is imperishable in me now stands face to face before Him Who Is." God is the only true keeper. Before, we imagined God's house, his keep, on some high mountain. But imagine instead God's house inside of you. Anything lodged there will never die. So make your prayer today, "Keep my life." And then read on to the end: "Hearken, O Lord, to my prayer, / and attend to the sound of my pleading."

Isaiah 58:9b–14
Psalm 86:1–2,3–4,5–6
Luke 5:27–32

Sunday

MARCH 5

• FIRST SUNDAY OF LENT •

At that time Jesus was led by the Spirit into the desert.
—MATTHEW 4:1

There was so much sand in all directions that it seemed like
air or water—not a thing in itself, just what contained
everything else. So it was the scattered stones, the only
objects in that barren landscape, that Jesus noticed. And
when the voice came, what else was there to talk about? Turn
these stones into bread, it said. Or send angels to save you
from dashing yourself on a rock. Jesus stayed seated among
the stones. And see these stones laid out like kingdoms? the
voice said. "All these I shall give to you." Yet it was not the
stones at all but the man who was the bread of life, the
stumbling block, the kingdom. So the voice disappeared, and
suddenly it was as if every stone became an angel and
gathered around the one who was and is the
everlasting Rock.

Genesis 2:7–9; 3:1–7
Psalm 51:3–4,5–6,12–13,17
Romans 5:12–19 or 5:12,17–19
Matthew 4:1–11

Amen, I say to you, whatever you did for one of these least brothers of mine, you did for me.
—MATTHEW 25:40

"We have all known the long loneliness," wrote the great social activist Dorothy Day, "and we have learned that the only solution is love and that love comes with community." If we look for God only in rarefied moments of prayer and beauty, then we'll almost entirely miss him. For God is in us, whom he calls the least of his brothers. "We cannot love God unless we love each other, and to love we must know each other," wrote Day. "We know Him in the breaking of bread, and we know each other in the breaking of bread, and we are not alone anymore." So look for God at the table—in church, at home, in the soup kitchen—anywhere there is, as Day put it, a crust of bread.

Leviticus 19:1–2,11–18
Psalm 19:8,9,10,15
Matthew 25:31–46

In praying, do not babble like the pagans, who think that they will be heard because of their many words.
—MATTHEW 6:7

Babbling is making sounds that have no meaning, and so often prayer feels like that to me. Words flood my thoughts—words of prayer, but also words of doubt, self-recrimination, and awkwardness—until it is all a jumble. The confusion of words crescendos in my head, not making much sense, until I can barely hear myself think. So I am grateful to be told, "This is how you pray." And yet how easy it is for memorized words to become rote, to prattle out unnoticed and unheard. Today, reflect on the words of the Lord's Prayer until they become your words. They are for you. For your Father, Jesus tells us, knows what you need before you ask him.

Isaiah 55:10–11
Psalm 34:4–5,6–7,16–17,18–19
Matthew 6:7–15

The queen of the south will rise with the men of this generation.
—LUKE 11:31

The queen of the south is the Queen of Sheba, a great
Ethiopian regent. Some say she was a fertility goddess. She
will rise, Jesus tells us, "because she came from the ends of
the earth to hear the wisdom of Solomon." Many have said
she simply represents the Church. These days we tend to
prefer symbolic interpretations, which don't get us tangled
up in history or science. But I prefer the medieval approach,
the belief that God wove metaphors into the tangible world.
A great queen could be both herself and a symbol. So when
Jesus says, "She will rise," I imagine that great resurrection,
when generations of people and saints and queens and gods
will come from the ends of the earth to see the one who is
the source of all symbol and truth.

Jonah 3:1–10
Psalm 51:3–4,12–13,18–19
Luke 11:29–32

Ask and it will be given to you;
seek and you will find.
—MATTHEW 7:7

This Gospel reading is paired with the story of Esther. "Now help me," Esther cries out, prostrate, "who am alone and have no one but you, O LORD, my God!" We know how her story ends. Help comes and her people are saved. And that is what we always want when we plead with God. We want real, physical change, fortunes and diseases reversed. But the last words of Esther's prayer help me think of help coming in a different way. Still pleading, she says, "Turn . . . our sorrows into wholeness." She could have said "into joy," but she said "wholeness." And that is exactly the aim of salvation, to make us whole. The process is slower than we'd like, but it is happening nonetheless, day by day, sorrow by sorrow.

Esther C:12,14–16,23–25
Psalm 138:1–2ab,2cde–3,7c–8
Matthew 7:7–12

My soul waits for the LORD
more than sentinels wait for the dawn.
—PSALM 130:6

Sentinels wait for that moment when they can finally go
home, when, as Zacharias says, "The dawn from on high
shall break upon us." Author and professor Anthony Esolen
points out that when Zacharias spoke these words, Jesus was
already alive in Mary's womb, and yet he said it *shall* break, as
if the dawn were still coming. "Christ is here, even in the
flesh," Esolen goes on, "in the sacrifice of the Mass, in this
Body the Church, in the witness of the saints, and in all the
graces God bestows upon us. He dwells among us, unto the
end of time. And yet, always, the greater and more glorious
dawn awaits." We are still in darkness. We are still waiting to
go home.

Ezekiel 18:21–28
Psalm 130:1–2,3–4,5–7a,7bc–8
Matthew 5:20–26

*He makes his sun rise on the bad and the good, and causes the rain to fall
on the just and the unjust.*
—MATTHEW 5:45

It has always bothered me that the tenets of Christianity
apparently exclude so many people. Once I went to a monk
with this concern. "Christ is real!" he said by way of
explanation. I think he meant that God is really there, not
just for believers but for everyone. St. Teresa of Ávila warned
her sisters that fretting over the souls of others can lead to
many mistakes. "So it is better," she told them, "to do what
our rule tells us—to try to live ever in silence and hope and
the Lord will take care of his own." We needn't worry that
our faith is leaving anyone out, for God makes his sun shine
on everyone, and he will take care of his own.

Deuteronomy 26:16–19
Psalm 119:1–2,4–5,7–8
Matthew 5:43–48

Christ Jesus . . . who destroyed death and brought life and immortality to light through the gospel.
—2 TIMOTHY 1:10

Even if we believe in life after death, we have no idea what that means. And yet throughout our lives we get these little flashes of insight, of what it might feel like to live forever. My copy of *The Secret Garden*, which I just finished reading to my children, is now tattered. I read it over and over as a child and marked several pages with big plastic clips. The clips are still there, the first one marking this passage: "One of the strange things about living in the world is that it is only now and then that one is quite sure one is going to live forever and ever and ever." And it makes me happy and makes me believe more to think that even as a child this mattered to me.

Genesis 12:1–4a
Psalm 33:4–5,18–19,20,22
2 Timothy 1:8b–10
Matthew 17:1–9

Be merciful, just as your Father is merciful.
Stop judging and you will not be judged. Stop condemning and you will
not be condemned.
Forgive and you will be forgiven.
—LUKE 6:36

Often, we overemphasize morality, and by focusing on it in ourselves we invariably notice immorality in others and begin to judge. Morality, as my husband puts it, is merely a concession to fallenness. We need it only because our desires lead us astray. Today we are told again and again—Jesus says it five different ways—that we will not be judged for our failure to keep the commandments but for our failure to forgive. "Yours, O Lord, our God, are compassion and forgiveness!" says Daniel today. Yes, we must try to be good, but in the end we will fail, and so will everyone else. The only way back is mercy.

Daniel 9:4b–10
Psalm 79:8,9,11 and 13
Luke 6:36–38

They tie up heavy burdens hard to carry and lay them on people's
shoulders, but they will not lift a finger to move them.
—MATTHEW 23:4

When Jesus accuses the Pharisees of laying burdens on
people's shoulders, I hear that other statement Jesus made
earlier in Matthew, "Take my yoke upon you." What is the
difference? In both cases the burden is hard to bear. When I
lost my first child, nearly the only relief I ever found from
sorrow was when others cried with me. Another time was at
her funeral, when, though I was still kneeling in my pew, I
had a sudden physical sensation of being carried. We don't
feel it always, that his yoke is easy and his burden light, but
when we do, we get a glimpse of the Resurrection, when
God lifted not just a finger but his entire life to move
our burdens.

Isaiah 1:10,16–20
Psalm 50:8–9,16bc–17,21 and 23
Matthew 23:1–12

Wednesday

MARCH 15

Can you drink the chalice that I am going to drink?
—MATTHEW 20:22

When my sister was about to give birth to her second child, her two-year-old son had a sudden regression. She was devastated and couldn't get out of bed. I flew from Chicago to be with her. I remember watching her son play on the floor, his small shoulders slumped away from me, his mind seemingly cut off from the outer world. He had forgotten even the little game he used to play with her locket. Now he is five years old. His autism still breaks her heart, but caring for him has transformed her life. And watching her has given me strength. We gain the courage to drink the chalice by watching other people drink and seeing that it's not just filled with sorrow but also with joy. And when sorrow comes our way, we in turn become someone else's courage.

Jeremiah 18:18–20
Psalm 31:5–6,14,15–16
Matthew 20:17–28

More torturous than all else is the human heart.
—JEREMIAH 17:9

This passage from Jeremiah is a description of hell, not a
place into which we'll be cast but a place inside of us. The
human heart turns away from the Lord and becomes, says
Jeremiah, like a barren bush in a salty and empty earth. With
such a tortured heart we might cry out, as it says in the
Gospel, "I am suffering torment in these flames." They are
flames of jealousy, bitterness, and anger. They could burn us
up if we're not careful. Today help comes as a warning: "If
they will not listen to Moses and the prophets, neither will
they be persuaded if someone should rise from the dead."
Now someone has risen from the dead—are we persuaded?
Will we still cling to our torment or stretch our roots out to
the stream, as Jeremiah says, and begin to live?

Jeremiah 17:5–10
Psalm 1:1–2,3,4 and 6
Luke 16:19–31

Hear another parable.
—MATTHEW 21:33

Today is the feast of St. Patrick. Everyone will be wearing shamrocks. As early as 1726, an account told of men tucking these clovers into their hats before heading to the pubs to "drown the shamrock." Now shamrocks are emblazoned with glitter on hats, flags, T-shirts, cake. For most, shamrocks are just another green symbol of Ireland. In Chicago, after dumping forty pounds of vegetable dye in the water, even the rivers run green. But it all began with St. Patrick's parable. He picked a clover and told some long-ago crowd that just as the *seamróg* is one plant with three leaves, God is one being with three persons. It may be hard to reconcile with the glitter and buckets of river dye, but like any great symbol, its overuse only speaks to its power. And the Trinity is there, whether or not we forget.

Genesis 37:3–4,12–13a,17b–28a
Psalm 105:16–17,18–19,20–21
Matthew 21:33–43,45–46

Saturday

MARCH 18

• ST. CYRIL OF JERUSALEM, BISHOP AND DOCTOR OF THE CHURCH •

Now we must celebrate and rejoice, because your brother was dead and has come to life again; he was lost and has been found.
—LUKE 15:32

All our attempts to forgive and be forgiven would seem futile, or at least tragic, if death were the final answer. But the story of the prodigal son makes a startling connection between forgiveness and resurrection. By forgiving each other, the story tells us, we are patching up what will ultimately be broken, while also helping to bring what was dead to life again. And in the story, it isn't just the life of the prodigal son, but the father who is also restored. Our lives are intertwined, so when someone is lost, part of us goes missing too. By forgiving, we gather each other back in and slowly come to life.

Micah 7:14–15,18–20
Psalm 103:1–2,3–4,9–10,11–12
Luke 15:1–3,11–32

Whoever drinks the water I shall give will never thirst; the water I shall
give will become in him a spring of water welling up to eternal life.
—JOHN 4:14

This image in this passage is somewhat like the parable of the
mustard seed. In that story a tiny seed grows into a tree, full
enough to harbor birds in its branches. Today we have a
spring, a small outlet of water that will eventually well up to
eternal life. It's reassuring to think that we don't begin with a
great, impressive faith; we begin with a little speck in our
palm or a trickle. These images also offer a way of thinking
about eternal life. Eternal life doesn't mean never dying, time
going around and around and never stopping, but a new kind
of existence in which the seed will have grown and the
trickle welled and we will have come into our fullness.

Exodus 17:3–7
Psalm 95:1–2,6–7,8–9
Romans 5:1–2,5–8
John 4:5–42 or 4:5–15,19b–26,39a,40–42

Monday

MARCH 20

• ST. JOSEPH, SPOUSE OF THE BLESSED VIRGIN MARY •

*Why were you looking for me? Did you not know that I must be in my
Father's house?*
—LUKE 2:49

When Joseph and Mary found their son in the temple, they'd
already been looking for him for days. They were panicked.
At first they felt only relief—and anger. "Son, why have you
done this to us?" Mary asked. I imagine Joseph frowning but
thankful beside her. But then Jesus said, "Did you not know I
must be in my Father's house?" And just like that, they lost
him again. Joseph had always known he wasn't Jesus' "real"
father, so maybe he was more prepared than Mary, but I
doubt it. Are any of us prepared for the day when our
children finally walk out the door and we have to accept that
they are no longer ours and in some sense never were? St.
Joseph, patron of families, pray for us.

2 Samuel 7:4–5a,12–14a,16
Psalm 89:2–3,4–5,27 and 29
Romans 4:13,16–18,22
Matthew 1:16,18–21,24a or Luke 2:41–51a

The Kingdom of heaven may be likened to a king who decided to settle accounts with his servants.
—MATTHEW 18:23

Today the parable says that if we forgive, we'll be forgiven. If we don't, then we'll be "handed over to the torturers." We're back to the tortured heart of last week. We've heard it again and again this Lent: we must forgive. Jesus practically screams it out today. Yet he knows we will fail. So he becomes like us, like the servant in today's parable, and is "handed over to his torturers until he should pay back the whole debt." He pays it back with his life. So what is the kingdom of heaven like? It is like a king who forgives his servant, and when the servant doesn't also learn how to forgive, the king sets out to be tortured in his place. He's there with us every time we fail.

Daniel 3:25,34–43
Psalm 25:4–5ab,6 and 7bc,8–9
Matthew 18:21–35

Wednesday

MARCH 22

I have come not to abolish but to fulfill.
—MATTHEW 5:17

To fulfill means to fill to the full, to supply what is lacking, to
bring a promise to completion—and what has he come to
fulfill? Everything. The myths, laws, mathematics,
civilization, stories, our lives—everything that has always
been insufficient and reached out for more. And yet we are
not fulfilled. Those who came before us looked forward in
hope. We who have come after look back in faith. We stand,
mirror images of each other, around this moment in history.
Every lacking, incomplete, promising thing that has ever
been is not abolished but reaches out, forward and back, to
the Incarnation and the Resurrection. Christ is the
fulfillment, but we are here, caught within time. To us he is
still being born and still rising, filling up the world like a
slow, imperceptible flood.

Deuteronomy 4:1,5–9
Psalm 147:12–13,15–16,19–20
Matthew 5:17–19

Thursday

MARCH 23

• ST. TURIBIUS DE MOGROVEJO, BISHOP •

Whoever is not with me is against me, and whoever does not gather with me scatters.
—LUKE 11:23

I recently read an essay by Holly Taylor, a convert from the Episcopal Church to Catholicism. Her central reason for converting was unity. Many churches fragment over conflict. But she claims that for a community to thrive, it must be committed to those it opposes. "In the mysterious calculus of the divine economy," she writes, unity "allows the possibility that it is precisely the love, the goodness, even of someone with whom I am at odds at the moment, that brings me to God." Salvation happens in community. When that community scatters, we lose bits of ourselves and some of the ways God planned to reach us. So we must gather together, despite our differences, for as Taylor says, "Our best chance may be hanging on to one another's heels."

Jeremiah 7:23–28
Psalm 95:1–2,6–7,8–9
Luke 11:14–23

You are not far from the Kingdom of God.
—MARK 12:34

Over a decade ago when I became Catholic, I felt like God lived at St. Gregory's church. I'd walk my dog and look up the street, trying to catch a glimpse of its red bricks, imagining God flickering in the sanctuary candle. Earlier, when I was little, I felt like God lived in the trees. Both times it was a sense that God was not far, just up the block or above our heads. But today Jesus tells a scribe he's not far from the kingdom because he's understood the centrality of loving God and loving your neighbor. In other words, the kingdom is present wherever love brings what is inside us into communion with what lies beyond. So if only I could hold these things together—my heart, the trees, the church—I think I would not be far indeed.

Hosea 14:2–10
Psalm 81:6c–8a,8bc–9,10–11ab,14 and 17
Mark 12:28–34

⇒ 118 ⇐

The Holy Spirit will come upon you, and the power of the Most High will overshadow you.
—LUKE 1:35

Today is one of the days when we feel the movement of the liturgical clock. It moves in quarters from Christmas to the Annunciation to Midsummer to Michaelmas. It also follows the celestial quarters. Christmas is the winter solstice, today is the vernal equinox. But since our liturgical year goes in a circle, different church times intersect with others. Today, in the middle of Lent, on the road to Calvary, the power of the Most High overshadows Mary, and Jesus is conceived. It's a quarter past Christmas, a quarter till Midsummer; our days and nights have equal length. We are weaving in and out of darkness, imagining we're getting closer to the end. But God's eternal time overlays ours, and in his eyes, even what is dying is also coming to life again.

Isaiah 7:10–14; 8:10
Psalm 40:7–8a,8b–9,10,11
Hebrews 10:4–10
Luke 1:26–38

Rabbi, who sinned, this man or his parents, that he was born blind?
—JOHN 9:2

The blind and deaf are often linked in people's minds. A
flustered hostess once handed my deaf in-laws a menu in
Braille. And at a retreat, my mother-in-law was inexplicably
paired with the only blind woman there, neither of them able
to follow the other's language. But my in-laws love being
deaf. And I love their deafness too. They speak with such
expressive vigor and slapstick humor, their hands flying
about like living words. And when they write in English,
their grammar is different, lively like their hands. "I am
thrilling," my mother-in-law says when she gets good news.
"No one sinned," Jesus says today, "it is so that the works of
God might be made visible." And my in-laws' beautiful
hands, drawing the vertical sign for God down their faces,
smashing an amen fist into a palm, do make God more visible
for me.

1 Samuel 16:1b,6–7,10–13a
Psalm 23:1–3a,3b–4,5,6 (1)
Ephesians 5:8–14
John 9:1–41 or 9:1,6–9,13–17,34–38

Lo, I am about to create a new heavens
and a new earth.
—ISAIAH 65:17

I love the idea of a working heaven, not a place of light and ecstasy but a place where we'd really want to live. In Ford Madox Ford's poem "On Heaven," he imagines heaven "in the cool of the even, after the burden and toil of the days, after the heat and haze, in the vine-hills." In Marilynne Robinson's novel *Housekeeping*, the grandmother pictures her destination "a measured distance away, standing in the ordinary light like some plain house." Isaiah gives another take: we'll live in the houses we build and eat the fruit of our vineyards and hear no sound of weeping. Immortality will feel like an old man rounding out his days. "He would be a very little God if he could not do all this," writes Ford, "and he is still the great God of all."

Isaiah 65:17–21
Psalm 30:2 and 4,5–6,11–12a and 13b
John 4:43–54

There is a stream whose runlets gladden the city of God,
the holy dwelling of the Most High.
God is in its midst; it shall not be disturbed.
—PSALM 46:5–6

We often vacation in Pennsylvania Amish country, close to where I grew up. We stay in a wood cabin at the end of Eli Road. When we drive in by night, only a single lamp burns at the back of every house, and other than that there are only stars and moonlight over the mountains and fields. If you sit outside, all you hear are birds and the creek. In my eyes, this place could be the city of God. And that creek, whose runlets certainly gladden our hearts and make the mountain ferns grow, no doubt has God in its midst. There's little quiet in Chicago, but thankfully we have Lake Michigan, which carries its own great silence, even while the city screams.

Ezekiel 47:1–9,12
Psalm 46:2–3,5–6,8–9
John 5:1–16

To those in darkness: Show yourselves!
—ISAIAH 49:9

My son is always afraid when he loses sight of me. I tell him I
could never forget him, ever, ever, but still he frantically
looks about. Even should "a mother forget her infant, . . . I
will never forget you," says the Lord. We are not children
anymore, and sometimes we'd prefer to be forgotten. But it
never works, because God knows where we are. "Come out!
You, who are in darkness," he calls. We look frantically
about. But he calls again, "Show yourselves!" And if you're
still not convinced, he tells us what it will be like. He will
come like a mother, full of tenderness and comfort and
mercy. I remember that feeling when I was little, finding
myself alone, maybe forgotten, and then there she was. I'd
run to her and feel nothing articulate, just those great arms
around me rocking me into peace.

Isaiah 49:8–15
Psalm 145:8–9,13cd–14,17–18
John 5:17–30

MARCH 30

But Moses, his chosen one,
Withstood him in the breach
to turn back his destructive wrath.
—PSALM 106:23

Today Moses appears in all the readings. In Exodus, he implores God not to let his wrath blaze against his people. In the psalm, Moses withstands God in the breach. But in the Gospel, Jesus tells us, "The one who will accuse you is Moses." What is going on? It seems to me that these readings show the passage from the Old Testament to the New. Moses brings us the law, which will ultimately accuse us, for we have not managed to keep it. But even as Moses lays down this incriminating law, he implores God to forgive us. And by doing so, he anticipates Christ, the one who will truly stand in the breach.

Exodus 32:7–14
Psalm 106:19–20,21–22,23
John 5:31–47

He watches over all his bones;
not one of them shall be broken.
—PSALM 34:20

When I picture my bones hidden beneath the surface, my mind recoils. The gaping eye sockets, the thin finger bones, the empty ribs mean only death, as if the Grim Reaper were waiting there under my skin. Today's reading is often used as a prophecy that Christ's bones will not be broken. But in the context of Psalm 34, God is speaking to us, his servants. And maybe these two interpretations aren't so far apart, for we are the body of Christ. We are God's bones. He watches over us, and even the brokenhearted, the psalm says, shall not be broken. So imagine yourself as God's bones, not a ghoulish skeleton but bone of his bone, that he formed to walk about the world and do his work.

Wisdom 2:1a,12–22
Psalm 34:17–18,19–20,21 and 23
John 7:1–2,10,25–30

Saturday

APRIL 1

Though I have fallen, I will arise.
—MICAH 7:8

This hope of arising makes me think of a beautiful story from chapter four of 2 Kings. A young boy gets a headache. "It's nothing big," his mother must have told herself. But later that day, "he died in her lap." She lays him on Elisha's bed and goes out. I remember that, watching myself turn away from my daughter's body and walk out into the blank day. Elisha places his mouth upon the child's mouth, his eyes upon the eyes, and his hands upon the hands. Earlier in the hospital, I tried to press the life of my body into my daughter's. And is that how it will be? Christ's body, his mouth, his eyes, his hands, pressed upon ours? And will he one day say to me, as Elisha said to the woman, "Take your child"? Resurrection is not some distant glory we'll never see. It's for us, for the mouths and eyes and hands we love.

OPTIONAL MASS:
Micah 7:7–9
Psalm 27:1,7–8a,8b–9abc,13–14
John 9:1–41

FOURTH WEEK OF LENT:
Jeremiah 11:18–20
Psalm 7:2–3,9bc–10,11–12
John 7:40–53

O my people! I will open up your graves and have you rise from them.
—EZEKIEL 37:12

Usually it is we who plead for our lives, bring our dying to healers, pray and wring our hands and grieve. But today God comes to us. "O my people!" he calls out, and in the Gospel Jesus kneels before the tomb of Lazarus and weeps. His act of grief exposes death for what it is, a tragedy. Once at a prayer service, for a woman who had watched her child die on the day of its birth, our pastor said, "Some people may say that your baby's death was God's will. Don't believe them. The God we worship, the God who watches over us, doesn't will the death of anyone." No, he grieves like we do and calls out to us and puts his spirit in us so that we may live.

Ezekiel 37:12–14
Psalm 130:1–2,3–4,5–6,7–8 (7)
Romans 8:8–11
John 11:1–45 or 11:3–7,17,20–27,33b–45

They suppressed their consciences; they would not allow their eyes to look to heaven.
—DANIEL 13:9

How often have I done that, refused to look to heaven, averted my eyes and gone my own way? I'm probably doing it right now. We build these dark little shelters around ourselves that obscure heaven. But there is one thing we can still do even in darkness. We can lay down the stone we almost heaved at someone else's shelter. Today Jesus says to the woman, "Has no one condemned you? Neither do I condemn you." It's terrifying to think we hold each other's condemnation in our hands like stones. Imagine it, the Apocalypse, all of us facing each other in a great circle, stones in hand, ready to kill. Or instead, imagine us laying down our stones and the darkness clearing. Our eyes would finally look up to a new heaven, and we'd walk out into a new earth.

Daniel 13:1–9,15–17,19–30,33–62 or 13:41c–62
Psalm 23:1–3a,3b–4,5,6
John 8:1–11

They said to him, "Who are you?"
Jesus said to them, "What I told you from the beginning."
—JOHN 8:25

When St. Augustine writes about this passage, it's as if all the
other words don't matter. "Who are you?" the Pharisees
asked. "The beginning," Jesus answered, or at least that's how
Augustine records it. And I see where Augustine gets this,
because two other times in today's reading, Jesus refers to
himself as "I AM." It's capitalized to make sure we get the
connection to the eternal name of God. "When you lift up
the Son of Man," Jesus says, "then you will realize that I AM."
He was there before the world began, and yet we lifted him
up and crucified him. But it was only through that act that we
understood who Jesus really was. Now we pray: as it was in
the beginning, is now and ever shall be, world without
end, amen.

Numbers 21:4–9
Psalm 102:2–3,16–18,19–21
John 8:21–30

Did we not cast three men bound into the fire?
—DANIEL 3:91

The three men were cast into the fire because the king told
them that every time they heard the sound of "the trumpet,
flute, lyre, harp, psaltery, bagpipe" they must worship an idol.
The men refused. I imagine the drone of the bagpipe starting
up and the hollow notes of a flute. And then the three men
being shackled and pushed into the white-hot furnace. Their
skin was supposed to blister and melt from their bodies. Yet
when the guards looked, they saw not three men but four, all
of them unfettered and one the Son of God. We will never
know in which atrocities Christ has appeared. But in our faith
in a loving God, we must assume it has been all of them.

Daniel 3:14–20,91–92,95
Daniel 3:52,53,54,55,56
John 8:31–42

APRIL 6

Jesus hid.
—JOHN 8:59

But right before Jesus hid, he said, "Amen, Amen, I say to you, before Abraham came to be, I AM." And everyone went crazy and picked up stones and looked for him, but he was gone. He became *Deus absconditus*, the hidden God, about whom theologians have written so much. In that small moment, we see a portrait of how we experience God. He is the eternal Father of the universe, and yet we don't see him. And sometimes we go crazy looking. "I want to climb up the blank blue dome as a man would storm the inside of a circus tent," writes Annie Dillard in her book *Pilgrim at Tinker Creek,* "wildly, dangling, and with a steel knife claw a rent in the top." And yet, it is only because he is hidden that we begin to look everywhere—in faces, in skies, in stones—and sometimes find him.

Genesis 17:3–9
Psalm 105:4–5,6–7,8–9
John 8:51–59

Friday

APRIL 7

• ST. JOHN BAPTIST DE LA SALLE, PRIEST •

It calls them gods to whom the word of God came.
—JOHN 10:35

Jesus is recounting Psalm 82 when the psalmist said, "I declare: 'gods though you be.'" Jesus explains what the psalmist meant, that anyone to whom the word of God comes is a god. And yet, the psalmist warned, "The gods neither know nor understand, / wandering about in darkness, / and all the world's foundations shake" (Psalm 82:5 NAB). Jesus must have been thinking about that part too, for he knew that soon he would die and the ground would shake and people would wander about in darkness. Easter is coming, and gods though we be, we do not understand and are not ready. All we can do is follow the psalmist, who also wrote, "Though I tried to understand all this, / it was too difficult for me, / till I entered the sanctuary of God" (73:16–17). Sometimes the only way to knowledge is by entering the mystery.

Jeremiah 20:10–13
Psalm 18:2–3a,3bc–4,5–6,7
John 10:31–42

What do you think? That he will not come to the feast?
—JOHN 11:56

The Passover was near and everyone was wondering, would Jesus show up? No one knew. Would he be seized and killed? Would God save him? The world held its breath. But it occurs to me that this question is also for us. It's the question of faith. Will Jesus show up at the altar or is it all a ruse? What do we believe? Lent is a time for conversion; every year we do it again, and no argument or evidence can answer the question for us. But even if the doubts still linger (for who said this was supposed to be easy?), we can still go forward in faith and show up at the feast.

Ezekiel 37:21–28
Jeremiah 31:10,11–12abcd,13
John 11:45–56

$\mathcal{S}unday$

APRIL 9

When he entered Jerusalem, the whole city was shaken and asked,
"Who is this?"
—MATTHEW 21:10

At first we join in with the disciples, waving our palm branches
and singing "Hosanna." I can't help hearing the *Jesus Christ
Superstar* version, "Hosanna, Hey Sanna," the heys and the hos
and the sannas cycling around, pointing out how little anyone
understood what was about to happen. Then we become the
angry mob calling for Jesus to die. And finally we are with
Peter, denying the Lord. We are called to enter this drama to
see that all those voices are still inside of us, each of us capable
of both worship and denial. So we might take a moment to
stand at the gates of Jerusalem and ask, "Who is this?" and
watch the figure, riding in on an ass, who has been the object
of so much hate and love through the centuries.

PROCESSION:
Matthew 21:1–11

MASS:
Isaiah 50:4–7
Psalm 22:8–9,17–18,19–20,23–24 (2a)
Philippians 2:6–11
Matthew 26:14–27:66 or 27:11–54

Monday

APRIL 10

• MONDAY OF HOLY WEEK •

You always have the poor with you, but you do not always have me.
—JOHN 12:8

It is tempting to always keep busy; there's so much to do and
there are so many in need. But the point of all this running
around is to support the real work of life. "You are anxious
and worried about many things," Jesus once told Martha,
who was "burdened with much serving." And then he said,
"There is need of only one thing." Mary, Martha's sister,
instead sat at his feet, and today she washes them with oil.
It's not easy to know how to direct our energies, but if our
busy lives, even lived in service to others, never allow us to
stop and be with the ones we love, then our purpose is
defeated. It is Holy Week, a time for contemplation. So take
a break from much serving and find the one thing that is
most needed.

Isaiah 42:1–7
Psalm 27:1,2,3,13–14
John 12:1–11

⇒ 135 ⇐

Tuesday

APRIL 11

• TUESDAY OF HOLY WEEK •

Hear me, O islands,
listen, O distant peoples.
—ISAIAH 49:1

There are two different movements in today's readings. First
there is a sense of arrival. Isaiah calls out, "Hear me, O
islands, / listen, O distant peoples." A light is coming, he
says, that will reach to the ends of the earth. And here we
are, a distant people, receiving this light. But there is also a
sense of departure. "My children," Jesus says gently, "I will be
with you only a little while longer." This double sense of
arrival and departure seems appropriate for us right now, for
we are approaching the Crucifixion, when leaving and
coming, sorrow and joy, will join together in a single act,
giving us hope that departure will someday turn into arrival
and sorrow into joy.

Isaiah 49:1–6
Psalm 71:1–2,3–4a,5ab–6ab,15 and 17
John 13:21–33,36–38

Wednesday

APRIL 12

• WEDNESDAY OF HOLY WEEK •

I have set my face like flint.
—ISAIAH 50:7

We are called to seek the presence of God, or *paniym* in Hebrew, which is also translated as "God's face." Yet we try to seek his face and see nothing. Isaiah tries to explain. In the voice of Christ, he says that he has set his face like flint. Flint is a kind of chert, a hard sedimentary rock, gray and blank. How easy it would be to overlook such a face, a face that could fade into the background, a face that could be anyone's. But flint has another property; when it's struck fire ignites. So look harder. His face could be anyone's. And if you look hard enough, you might not have to wait until tragedy or hardship strikes and reveals Christ's presence burning in the face of your neighbor, your friend, yourself.

Isaiah 50:4–9a
Psalm 69:8–10,21–22,31 and 33–34
Matthew 26:14–25

[Jesus] unrolled the scroll and found the passage where it was written:
The Spirit of the Lord is upon me,
because he has anointed me.
—LUKE 4:17–18

Again we are told of the beginning as we approach the end.
Years ago, when I held my baby who died shortly before
birth, the beginning and the end came starkly together. Holy
Thursday feels like that to me. For today we bless both the
oil of baptism and of the sick, and the priest washes the feet
of the very young and the old. Surely, even with no religion,
we would still anoint our newly born and dead, if only with
our tears. But we have a church that fills these anointings
with the Spirit of the Lord, and we are left not to merely bear
life but also to hope that the One who so determined our
beginning will not fail us at the end.

CHRISM MASS:	EVENING MASS OF THE LORD'S SUPPER:
Isaiah 61:1–3a,6a,8b–9	Exodus 12:1–8,11–14
Psalm 89:21–22,25,27	Psalm 116:12–13,15–16bc,17–18
Revelation 1:5–8	1 Corinthians 11:23–26
Luke 4:16–21	John 13:1–15

Friday

APRIL 14

• FRIDAY OF THE PASSION OF THE LORD (GOOD FRIDAY) •

What is truth?
—JOHN 18:38

I've been watching reruns of the new *Cosmos*, a miniseries that explores concepts about space. It's stunning, epic, and I would love it completely if it weren't for the intermittent commentary that goes something like this: Once people thought comets *meant* something. Now because we know the truth, that they are frozen balls of gas and dust, we know they mean nothing. Again and again scientific explanation is used to eradicate meaning. They can pull it off in a show about stars and molecules, but if the topic were love or death or forgiveness, would we still buy it? Today Jesus says, "For this I was born, . . . to testify to the truth." And Pontius Pilate, the rationalist, the scientist, asks, "What is truth?" and does not stay for an answer. But we can look through history and still see Truth standing there alone, in his crown of thorns and purple robe.

Isaiah 52:13–53:12
Psalm 31:2,6,12–13,15–16,17,25
Hebrews 4:14–16; 5:7–9
John 18:1–19:42

Saturday

APRIL 15

• HOLY SATURDAY •

*I will give you a new heart and place a new spirit within you, taking
from your bodies your stony hearts and giving you natural hearts.*
—EZEKIEL 36:26

The Easter Vigil begins in darkness with the Exsultet, that
grand hymn of praise sung before the paschal candle. It calls
out to all corners of the earth. *This is the night*, it repeats. *This is
the night, dazzling and full of gladness.* And more than any other
night, I feel myself lifted out of the gloom, out of the stoniness,
and can sing out, "He is risen" and believe it. There is little talk
of what has held us back; we assume it all—that we are here,
we've come to the feast, and *this is the night*. This is the night we
have natural hearts, the way they were meant to be, in
communion with the ends of the earth, and full of gladness.

EASTER VIGIL:
Genesis 1:1–2:2 or 1:1,26–31a
Psalm 104:1–2,5–6,10,12,13–14,24,35 or
33:4–5,6–7,12–13,20–22
Genesis 22:1–18 or 22:1–2,9a,10–13,15–18
Psalm 16:5,8,9–10,11
Exodus 14:15–15:1
Exodus 15:1–2,3–4,5–6,17–18
Isaiah 54:5–14
Psalm 30:2,4,5–6,11–12,13

Isaiah 55:1–11
Isaiah 12:2–3,4,5–6
Baruch 3:9–15,32–4:4
Psalm 19:8,9,10,11
Ezekiel 36:16–17a,18–28
Psalm 42:3,5; 43:3,4 or Isaiah 12:2–3,4bcd,5–6
or Psalm 51:12–13,14–15,18–19
Romans 6:3–11
Psalm 118:1–2,16–17,22–23
Matthew 28:1–10

Stay with us, for it is nearly evening and the day is almost over.
—LUKE 24:29

We can bear almost anything during the day; the light keeps us afloat. But then the sun goes down. The disciples were reeling with grief. Just three days before at Calvary, they had wept and clawed the earth. Now they walked about in dumb confusion, traumatized and lost. Then out of nowhere a man appeared. They clung to his words and begged him to stay. And he did. He broke the bread and gave it to them, and they saw who he was and then he vanished from sight. If they'd known he was about to leave, they would have said it again: "Stay with us." And we are like them. It's so difficult to hold on to belief. It can slip away quick as the sun. So Lord, stay with us, the day is almost over.

Acts 10:34a,37–43
Psalm 118:1–2,16–17,22–23
Colossians 3:1–4 or 1 Corinthians 5:6b–8
John 20:1–9 or Matthew 28:1–10 or (at an afternoon or evening Mass) Luke 24:13–35

They approached, embraced his feet, and did him homage.
—MATTHEW 28:9

I remember the radiologist telling me it's the foot she loves to
find in utero. I didn't understand this until my babies were
born. Then I found myself kissing and cradling their feet
almost as much as their heads. And recently, visiting my
mother, I noticed her reach down and touch my foot. She's
probably done this a thousand times, but this time I watched
and realized that that tenderness never goes away. It made
me ache for my mother and for my children. Touching feet is
a gesture of respect in some countries as automatic as shaking
hands is to us. But behold, when Jesus, who had died, met
Mary Magdalene and Mary on their way to announce the
news to the disciples, I doubt it was respect foremost that
caused them to embrace his feet, but something more akin to
the brokenhearted love of a mother.

Acts 2:14,22–33
Psalm 16:1–2a and 5,7–8,9–10,11
Matthew 28:8–15

Jesus said to her, "Mary!"
She turned and said to him in Hebrew, "Rabbouni," which
means Teacher.
—JOHN 20:16

Their conversation didn't start in that way. First, Jesus called her "woman." "Woman, why are you weeping?" he asked. And she addressed him "Sir." But then the tone changed. "Mary," he said. And when she heard her name she knew it was him. I imagine her voice softening to a whisper. "Rabbouni," she said. It's the only time this word appears in Scripture. Some say it's merely a synonym for *rabbi*, but others say it's closer to "my dear, sweet teacher, my own." This makes sense to me, for Jesus goes on in this way. "I am going to my Father," he says. Then he gently adds, "And your Father. To my God and your God." And someday he will come for us like this too and call us by name.

Acts 2:36–41
Psalm 33:4–5,18–19,20 and 22
John 20:11–18

And a man crippled from birth was carried and placed at the gate of the temple called "the Beautiful Gate" every day.
—ACTS 3:2

I just finished a book by Katherine Boo called *Behind the Beautiful Forevers*, about a slum in Mumbai. The title comes from a giant billboard that marks the edge of the makeshift settlement. In sunshine yellow, the sign advertises ceramic tiles by repeating the words "Beautiful" and "Forever." Today's reading has a similar irony. The lame and deformed and hungry gather under "the Beautiful Gate." But it's only ironic to those who can't see beyond what people look like on the surface. Peter walked right up to the crippled man and "looked intently at him" and saw the man's "jumping and praising" spirit. So he "took him by the right hand and raised him up." The man stood and walked around and everyone else could finally see what the gate had already proclaimed.

Acts 3:1–10
Psalm 105:1–2,3–4,6–7,8–9
Luke 24:13–35

Touch me and see, because a ghost does not have flesh and bones as you can see I have.
—LUKE 24:39

"Why do questions arise in your heart?" Jesus asks the disciples. And he shows them his hands and feet and says, "It is I myself." I read this and wonder what reassurance there is for us, for he is not standing here now in the flesh. But when I think of the moments in my life that have convinced me of eternity, they are precisely those that involve both touching and seeing. Intense love or tenderness, the eyes and the body unable to take in enough, make death seem impossible and resurrection an almost inevitable consequence of love. So the reassurance is this: he once stood before a crowd of people like us, but he stands here still, he himself, in those we love.

Acts 3:11–26
Psalm 8:2ab and 5,6–7,8–9
Luke 24:35–48

Friday

APRIL 21

• FRIDAY WITHIN THE OCTAVE OF EASTER •

When Simon Peter heard that it was the Lord, he tucked in his garment,
for he was lightly clad, and jumped into the sea.
—JOHN 21:7

Simon Peter could bear it no more. "I am going fishing," he
announced, hoping the water and sky and boat might make
his life feel like it used to feel, hard and human and good, not
this gaping grief. They fished all day and caught nothing. So
when a man told them to cast their net in again and they
couldn't haul it up for the weight, Peter wouldn't believe it.
"It is the Lord," said John. And then, with that old fire and
conviction, Peter hurled himself into the sea. When he
reached the shore dripping and astonished, Jesus said simply,
"Come, have breakfast." It's so like what I hope for. No choir
of angels, just a return to that hard, good, human life.

Acts 4:1–12
Psalm 118:1–2 and 4,22–24,25–27a
John 21:1–14

Go into the whole world and proclaim the Gospel to every creature.
—MARK 16:15

Some say this should read "to all creation" instead, but I like the more explicit suggestion that even animals profit from the good news. In an article against a heaven with no animals, theologian David Bentley Hart writes, "I, in contrast, hope to see puppies in paradise, and persevere in faith principally for that reason." The desire for us to be accompanied in eternity is a deep one. Recently, in a museum, my daughter stopped short before a painting of a Mexican village. On a staircase spiraling out of a cemetery into the clouds was a procession of men and beasts. "Look," she said triumphantly, "dogs do go to heaven," as if this artist's vision decided it. And then of course there's St. Francis, who unabashedly proclaimed the Gospel to Brother Wolf and Sister Bird.

Acts 4:13–21
Psalm 118:1 and 14–15ab,16–18,19–21
Mark 16:9–15

Sunday

APRIL 23

• SECOND SUNDAY OF EASTER (OR SUNDAY OF DIVINE MERCY) •

They ate their meals with exultation and sincerity of heart.
—ACTS 2:46

Awe had recently come upon the disciples, it says in Acts, and this was the result. It reminds me of Isak Dinesen's story "Babette's Feast." A mysterious French chef prepares a feast for a tiny, pious community in Denmark. Despite their religion and ascetic ways, these people are sinners like everyone else, and they have long-held grudges and bitterness. But as the magical feast wears on, the vain illusion of this world dissolves before their eyes like smoke, and they are given one hour of the millennium. And in a way, they don't wonder at this infinite grace, Dinesen says, for it was but the fulfillment of an ever-present hope. We may be full of bitterness, we may still tend our grudges, but even so hope is working in us, readying us for the feast.

Acts 2:42–47
Psalm 118:2–4,13–15,22–24
1 Peter 1:3–9
John 20:19–31

Monday

APRIL 24

• ST. FIDELIS OF SIGMARINGEN, PRIEST AND MARTYR •

How can a man once grown old be born again? Surely he cannot reenter
his mother's womb and be born again, can he?
—JOHN 3:4

These are the honest questions of Nicodemus, a Pharisee. He
appears only in the Gospel of John. First there is this
conversation about being born of the Spirit. But even after
Jesus explains, Nicodemus still asks, "How can this happen?"
And that's the last we hear of him until he calmly urges the
Sanhedrin to hear the testimony of Jesus before judging.
Finally he brings myrrh and aloe for Jesus' burial. I'm grateful
to John for including this sketch of Nicodemus and grateful
to the Church for making him a saint, for Nicodemus gives
us a portrait of faith I find encouraging. What do we know of
him? Nicodemus was full of questions, he was prudent, and in
the end, he came to worship.

Acts 4:23–31
Psalm 2:1–3,4–7a,7b–9
John 3:1–8

Tuesday

APRIL 25

• ST. MARK, EVANGELIST •

They will pick up serpents with their hands,
and if they drink any deadly thing,
it will not harm them.
—MARK 16:18

The disciples are not invincible; all but one will be martyred.
So what does Jesus mean by saying the disciples will handle
snakes and drink poison without harm? Moses had once
lifted up a serpent on a staff and healed the snakebites of
God's people. In the Gospel of John, Jesus referred to this,
saying, "Just as Moses lifted up the serpent in the desert, so
must the Son of Man be lifted up" (3:14 NAB). It's a startling
analogy, likening a snake on a staff to God crucified on a
tree. But in both cases, the curse became the cure. Only by
looking upon the snake would you be healed. Only by dying
could death be overcome. The disciples will be nailed to
crosses, cut with saws and knives, and drowned, but in some
real sense, they will not be harmed.

1 Peter 5:5b–14
Psalm 89:2–3,6–7,16–17
Mark 16:15–20

Go and take your place in the temple area, and tell the people everything about this life.
—ACTS 5:20

The angel says these words, throwing open the doors of the prison. In his classic *Exposition of the Bible*, theologian John Gill says that "everything about this life" is simply the Word of Life and "the means of quickening dead sinners and reviving drooping saints." But to me everything about this life seems even more encompassing. Imagine it being said to you: *tell everything about this life.* It is a call to witness, to share our stories. For as people of faith, the story of our life, even a life full of doubt and sorrow and failure, tells the story of our journey to God. And by hearing one another's stories, we are reminded that our story is not yet finished, that we are still on the way. So all you drooping saints, revive! Your story is not over.

Acts 5:17–26
Psalm 34:2–3,4–5,6–7,8–9
John 3:16–21

APRIL 27

He does not ration his gift of the Spirit.
—JOHN 3:34

When I read this passage, I imagine those World War II ration queues, with people lining up for their measure, their tin of dry milk, their packet of suet and a few ounces of tea. How different from God's good measure, pressed down, shaken together, and running over, poured into our laps. God does not ration his gifts, but we ration ours. And in some sense we must. We have only a fixed amount of energy, time, money, life. But then again, God isn't pouring time and money into our laps either. I did a word search for "God gives" in Scripture. From Genesis to Revelation, it tells of what God gives: breath, rest, light, wisdom, strength, peace, love. When we queue up in Mass to receive our tiny scrap of bread, our sip of wine, it's not a ration but this abundance that awaits.

Acts 5:27–33
Psalm 34:2 and 9,17–18,19–20
John 3:31–36

Friday

APRIL 28

• ST. PETER CHANEL, PRIEST AND MARTYR • ST. LOUIS GRIGNION DE MONTFORT, PRIEST •

There is a boy here who has five barley loaves and two fish.
—JOHN 6:9

Once I was singled out in school. A Journey cover band had come to perform. Crowded into the gym bleachers, we watched these wannabe rockers with wry, teenage amusement. But then the lead singer, shaggy hair and tight jeans, picked me out of the crowd. I stood there red-faced in front of everyone while he sang on bended knee. Though I never would've admitted it, I went home and swooned. I know it's silly, but I thought of this when I read today's Gospel, the boy standing there, singled out, watching his bread and loaves feed the multitude. Did his cheeks burn? Did he even eat? But when Jesus snuck away to "withdraw to the mountain," I bet he watched, and later, lying in his bed, pictured that mountain as if it were his and wished he could go.

Acts 5:34–42
Psalm 27:1,4,13–14
John 6:1–15

When they had rowed about three or four miles, they saw Jesus walking
on the sea and coming near the boat.
—JOHN 6:19

"I conclude that miracles do happen," the theologian G. K.
Chesterton wrote, for "the men who encounter elves or
angels are not the mystics and the morbid dreamers, but
fishermen, farmers, and all men at once course and careful."
Course and careful, the disciples couldn't believe Jesus was
really doing it, walking on the sea. Maybe it was some sort of
forward energy, like a skipping rock, and any minute he'd
plunge beneath the waves. Course and careful, they tried to
take him into the boat, but then "the boat immediately
arrived at the shore to which they were heading." Even then,
did they just chalk it up to the storm and tide? They resisted
miracles as much as we do, but by giving us these course and
careful accounts they shored up our belief.

Acts 6:1–7
Psalm 33:1–2,4–5,18–19
John 6:16–21

God raised this Jesus; of this we are all witnesses.
—ACTS 2:32

The wording of today's readings points out the singularity of
Jesus. Peter calls him not just Jesus but *this* Jesus. Of *this* we
are all witnesses. And then in the psalm, instead of saying,
"You are my Lord," David says, "My Lord are you." Later,
instead of "It is you," he adds, "You it is who hold fast my lot."
The emphasis of these sentences captures the scandal of
Christianity. So many people today prefer to have faith in
something obviously huge and unspecified, so they pray to
the universe as if it were God. But we instead have poured all
of our faith into a single person. We believe that in all the
dark universe it is this Jesus, Our Lord, him it is, who holds
fast our lot.

Acts 2:14,22–33
Psalm 16:1–2,5,7–8,9–10,11 (11a)
1 Peter 1:17–21
Luke 24:13–35

Monday

MAY 1

• ST. JOSEPH THE WORKER •

All those who sat in the Sanhedrin looked intently at him and saw that his face was like the face of an angel.

—ACTS 6:15

We tend to assume that the world we see can be described in clear, objective ways. We tend to think that the record of our senses—what we see and hear and touch—will square up with science. But today's reading points out that this isn't always the case. The people sitting in the Sanhedrin that day looked upon a real human face and saw something they didn't understand. What was it like? A gleam? Some veiled radiance? That day a whole roomful of skeptics looked upon Stephen's face and could think of no earthly way to describe it. "His face," they said, reaching beyond the known, reaching for what they could only intuit, "was like the face of an angel."

Acts 6:8–15
Psalm 119:23–24,26–27,29–30
John 6:22–29 (or, for the Memorial, Genesis
1:26–2:3 or Colossians 3:14–15,17,23–24)
Psalm 90:2,3–4,12–13,14 and 16
Matthew 13:54–58

Tuesday

MAY 2

• ST. ATHANASIUS, BISHOP AND DOCTOR OF THE CHURCH •

*What sign can you do, that we may see and believe in you? What
can you do?*
—JOHN 6:30

The crowd is begging him. Don't make us have faith. Show
us some incontrovertible sign that will prove it's all true.
Maybe bread falling down from the skies? they helpfully
suggest. But Jesus says it doesn't work that way. What you
need is the bread that comes down from heaven and gives
life to the world, he says. And then the clincher, "I am the
bread." They murmur among themselves. "Stop murmuring,"
he says. "I am the bread of life," come the impossible words,
"whoever eats this bread will live forever" (John
6:41,43,48,51 NAB). There's no way around it. Sure, bread
can fall from the skies and men walk on water, but that's
beside the point. Life, eternal life, requires belief. We are
called to it every time we come to the altar.

Acts 7:51–8:1a
Psalm 31:3cd–4,6 and 7b and 8a,17 and 21ab
John 6:30–35

⋛ 157 ⋚

Wednesday

MAY 3

• SS. PHILIP AND JAMES, APOSTLES •

The Father who dwells in me is doing his works.
—JOHN 14:10

The entire reading from John today is about salvation and
how it stems from the will of God. "And this is the will of the
one who sent me," Jesus says earlier in John, "that I should
not lose anything of what he gave me, but that I should raise
it on the last day" (6:39 NAB). He uses that tiny word "it" to
hold all of us, or at least that's what we hope he meant.
"Often we think of hope in too individualistic a manner, as
merely our personal salvation," wrote Cardinal Jean
Daniélou. "In reality hope bears on the salvation of all
men—and it is only in the measure that I am immersed in
them that it bears on me." It is not wrong to hope that none
will be lost, that all will be saved. In fact, the only way to
participate in our own salvation is to hope that that tiny
word, *it*, like a single hand, is indeed big enough to hold
us all.

1 Corinthians 15:1–8
Psalm 19:2–3,4–5
John 14:6–14

Look, there is water. What is to prevent my being baptized?
—ACTS 8:36

Was the water a pond, a stream, a puddle? The passage says that they "went down into the water," so it must have been a significant body. Yet the urgency of this baptism—*look, there is water*—gives me the sense that even a tiny pool would've done the trick. I like to imagine the Ethiopian court official stepping out of his chariot, no water in any direction but for a rut in the road filled with rainwater, and Philip stooping down to lift a handful of muddy water over his head, and then going forth rejoicing. This scene gives us a vision of the world sanctified: God spread out in all the world's waters, the dew and puddles and seas standing in wait. What is to prevent a blessing?

Acts 8:26–40
Psalm 66:8–9,16–17,20
John 6:44–51

Friday

MAY 5

Immediately things like scales fell from his eyes.
—ACTS 9:18

I recently discovered that our eyes are closely related to the eyes of fish. And that some fish can see better underwater—farther and more clearly—than we can see through air. But it's interesting, children of the Chinese Tanka people, or "boat people," often spend so much time immersed in the ocean that they develop superior underwater vision. Today, Saul's normal vision is interrupted. The sky suddenly flashes around him, and when he opens his eyes he can see nothing. Later, after baptism, he regains his sight. This passage shows his physical sight reflecting his inner ability to see. But Saul's transformation also reflects the actual workings of eyes. For it is only by being immersed in water that he can truly see. And what a beautiful conception of baptism: that afterward we see through a kind of spiritual water rather than plain, unsanctified air.

Acts 9:1–20
Psalm 117:1bc,2
John 6:52–59

The Church throughout all Judea, Galilee, and Samaria was at peace.
She was being built up and walked in the fear of the Lord.
—ACTS 9:31

Many people balk at the dominant use of the masculine in
Scripture, woman coming from a man's rib no less. But today
the Church is described as a woman. It's similar to how
Sirach describes wisdom. He says that she will walk with us
and that he who holds her fast inherits glory. But this
feminine description also sounds like a reference to the Son.
And Sirach says that she breathes life into her children. But
this makes me think of the Father. Throughout Scripture, the
masculine and feminine intertwine. God is a hen brooding
over her young. God is a mother. And then there is Mary,
who is both the "model of the Church" and "seat of wisdom,"
and out of whose body God came.

Acts 9:31–42
Psalm 116:12–13,14–15,16–17
John 6:60–69

When he was insulted, he returned no insult; when he suffered, he did not threaten.
—1 PETER 2:23

Ever since I was little, getting hurt has made me angry. My sister is even more extreme. When she was a toddler, instead of crying she'd be furious, holding her breath, turning blue with rage, and once even passing out. Just yesterday, when my friend inadvertently stepped on her four-year-old's foot, I watched his face darken and his little fists fly out to hit her. It's our animal nature that snarls and spits. But there was one man who returned no insult and did not threaten. Only by his example have others managed to follow in his footsteps.

Gandhi, one such follower, says this of Jesus: "I refuse to believe that there now exists or has ever existed a person that has not made use of his example, . . . [not] been changed by his presence."

Acts 2:14a,36–41
Psalm 23:1–3a,3b–4,5,6 (1)
1 Peter 2:20b–25
John 10:1–10

I am the good shepherd.
—JOHN 10:11

My children and I have just gotten to the part in Laura Ingalls Wilder's *Little House on the Prairie* when Pa builds their house. "This is a country I'll be contented to stay in," he declares. "This country'll never feel crowded. Look at that sky!" At night the sky is "like a bowl of light overturned on the flat black land." It's an image of space and light. Today Jesus is talking about a sheepfold. I picture those crowded pens, the sheep being herded in, their bodies pressed so close together they look like a solid mass of undifferentiated wool. Earlier in John, Jesus said, "I am the gate" but added that whoever enters "will come in and go out and find pasture" (10:9). By passing through this gate, we are not trapped but let out into a wider, brighter, freer country.

Acts 11:1–18
Psalm 42:2–3; 43:3,4
John 10:11–18

The feast of the Dedication was taking place in Jerusalem. It was winter.
—JOHN 10:22

Ever since Easter Sunday, the readings have been trying to help us understand who Jesus was. I feel a certain solidarity with the early Christians, who were trying to wrap their heads around the same thing. They went over and over his various declarations. But it was never abstract reporting. It mattered that Jesus stood in a particular location and time. Today, this is their report: it was the Feast of Dedication, or Hanukkah, in Jerusalem. It was winter. Jesus walked about in the temple area of the Portico of Solomon and said, "The Father and I are one." The early Christians repeated this story and finally wrote it down. And now we stand with them in awe that once someone walked about, a real man, in a real place, and declared he was God.

Acts 11:19–26
Psalm 87:1b–3,4–5,6–7
John 10:22–30

Wednesday

MAY 10

• ST. DAMIEN DE VEUSTER, PRIEST •

They returned to Jerusalem, taking with them John, who is called Mark.
—ACTS 12:25

This line from the reading for today startled me for entirely personal reasons. People often confuse my son's name with my husband's. My son is John but is often called Mark. Today the reading from Acts mentions two ways of being called: the names we are called by and the work we are called to. The poet and animal trainer Vicki Hearne believes these two ways of being called are deeply connected. Names are not just labels, she says, but real calls or vocations. "Not only did Adam name the animals," says Hearne, "but the moment he did, each recognized his or her name . . . and came when called." From the day we are born, our names call us into our lives. And it makes sense to me that my son would feel a double calling: becoming himself, becoming John, and becoming his father, whom he loves.

Acts 12:24–13:5a
Psalm 67:2–3,5,6 and 8
John 12:44–50

Thursday

MAY 11

Amen, amen, I say to you, whoever receives the one I send receives me.
—JOHN 13:20

This alternation between receiving and sending is the central
cycle of our faith. God sends Jesus into the world. Jesus sends
us. Anyone who receives us also receives Jesus and so
receives God, and the cycle is complete. But it's not just a
matter of sending. Jesus says all this as he stoops to wash the
disciples' feet. Imagine God stooping there before you,
letting water fall from his hands over your feet. "No servant is
greater than his master," he says, looking up at you, "nor any
messenger greater than the one who sent him." Incredibly, he
is the servant, kneeling at your feet. Mass—a word that
means "sending forth"—is the repetition of this cycle. Every
Sunday we receive the body of Christ and then are sent forth
to go in peace to love and serve the Lord.

Acts 13:13–25
Psalm 89:2–3,21–22,25 and 27
John 13:16–20

Friday

MAY 12

Master, we do not know where you are going; how can we know the way?
—JOHN 14:5

Thomas wants a map and a compass. So do I. But Jesus answers him, "I am the way." A way, though, is a direction or destination, not usually a person. But our word comes from the German *weg*, which means "to move" or "to carry." "I will come back again and take you to myself," Jesus says, "so that where I am you also may be." This must be why I love tales of fairy roads, those sudden paths that open up where once there'd been nothing. Bordered by high hawthorn hedges, as fantasy writer Susanna Clarke imagines them, they are dim and shadowy, barely revealing the person with thistledown hair coming to lead us to the dance. We are being beckoned, carried, always by the Way that is both direction and destination and that moves the world.

Acts 13:26–33
Psalm 2:6–7,8–9,10–11ab
John 14:1–6

⋛ 167 ⋚

Saturday

MAY 13

• OUR LADY OF FATIMA •

Master, show us the Father, and that will be enough for us.
—JOHN 14:8

"Just the Father," says Philip, and I can't help hearing the disciples as characters in Monty Python's *Life of Brian* with cockney accents. "You know, maker of heaven and earth," they'd say. "That's all we need, just God Almighty. That'll be enough." Jesus must have looked at Philip before responding. For there he was, God himself, standing in the midst of his own creation, sun on the clouds, wind in the trees. "Have I been with you for so long a time and you do not know me, Philip?" he asks. "I am in the Father and the Father is in me." He offers Philip not a proof but himself. And it's what he offers us, too. Maybe if we stop being so flabbergasted and quiet down, still our hearts, we'll finally see what is already before our eyes.

Acts 13:44–52
Psalm 98:1,2–3ab,3cd–4
John 14:7–14

Beloved: Come to him, a living stone, rejected by human beings but chosen and precious in the sight of God.
—1 PETER 2:4

Last year I took my son and goddaughter to Chicago's Field Museum. The highlight of the trip for them was a hallway case of gemstones. Both children peered in and simultaneously gasped. "A ruby," they whispered. I'm sure I would have walked right past it, on to something more obviously startling, the dinosaurs or the Egyptian tomb, but instead I peered in with them and tried to imagine their thoughts. They've both been steeped in fairy tales, and to them the world of kings and queens and magic lands is not dead. They gazed in awe at the stone as if it had been plucked right out of legend. It's this kind of sight we must try to reclaim, to believe again that majesty and kingdoms and living stones are indeed possible.

Acts 6:1–7
Psalm 33:1–2,4–5,18–19 (22)
1 Peter 2:4–9
John 14:1–12

The gods have come down to us in human form.
—ACTS 14:11

People have always longed to see and touch God. So when
the disciples healed a man who was crippled since birth, the
people of Lystra called them Zeus and Hermes and rushed
forth with oxen and garlands. But the disciples cried out, "We
are of the same nature as you, human beings." But still the
people pressed forward with flowers, desperate to worship.
Maybe the people of Lystra weren't yet sure whom they were
worshiping, but it seems to me that our church has gotten
over the disciples' initial shock and embraced the need for
physical worship: to look upon, touch, kneel, bring gifts, and
feast. Is it really that strange, after all, to hope for God to
come down to us in human form?

Acts 14:5–18
Psalm 115:1–2,3–4,15–16
John 14:21–26

*Peace I leave with you; my peace I give to you. Not as the world gives
do I give it to you.*
—JOHN 14:27

We hear the first part in every Mass, but not the second, or
what comes next. "I am going away," Jesus says, and later,
"You will weep and mourn" (John 16:20 NAB). It's easy to
forget all this and treat the moment as purely social, smiling
and shaking hands without a thought. "I have told you this so
that you might have peace in me," he concludes. "In the
world you will have trouble, but take courage, I have
conquered the world" (John 16:33). The peace we offer one
another is not meant to be a happy wave across the pews. It's
meant to be a battle cry, calling us to grasp hands, especially
with those in fresh pain, and take courage.

Acts 14:19–28
Psalm 145:10–11,12–13ab,21
John 14:27–31a

MAY 17

Remain in me, as I remain in you.
—JOHN 15:4

For the past few days Jesus has been leading up to this passage. "I am in the Father and the Father is in me," he said on Saturday. And on Monday, "Whoever loves me will keep my word . . . and we will come to him and make our dwelling with him." We usually imagine that we are alone, inescapably alone in our bodies and minds. But here Jesus is saying it's not like that. Love allows us to remain or abide in God and God in us. And *remain* also carries that sense of staying even after something or someone has gone. It whispers to us of what lies beyond death. We are not alone, and we don't have to someday depart. Instead, through love and the keeping of words, we can forever remain in God, as God remains in us.

Acts 15:1–6
Psalm 122:1–2,3–4ab,4cd–5
John 15:1–8

Thursday

MAY 18

• ST. JOHN I, POPE AND MARTYR •

Remain in my love.
—JOHN 15:9

"Remain in my love," Jesus says again today, imploring us not to drift away. And later he prays for our salvation, "I in them and you in me, that they may be brought to perfection as one" (John 17:23 NAB). He's praying for the end of time when we will all be in communion with each other and with God. Pope Benedict puts it like this: "The individual will break through the limits of being into the whole and the whole take up its dwelling in the individual." It's been weeks since Easter. The joy and conviction of the Resurrection are wearing thin. But even as we make our way back to our lonely lives, this great love still calls to us, "Remain."

Acts 15:7–21
Psalm 96:1–2a,2b–3,10
John 15:9–11

Friday

MAY 19

It was not you who chose me, but I who chose you.
—JOHN 15:16

I have a fond little dialogue with my husband. I ask, "How did I ever find you?" And he says, "No, but I found you." In Randall Jarrell's tale *The Animal Family*, there's a similar exchange. A mermaid and a hunter build an odd family. First a bear comes, then a lynx, and then a little orphaned boy. They always tell the boy he was found by the lynx. And the boy says, "No, I was always with you." It becomes a game, and they reverse it. "Remember when the lynx found me?" asks the boy. "But you've been with us always," they say. They say it, Jarrell says, because it makes them happy, and, "well, for so many reasons." Today we might ask, "Lord, how did we find you?" And he would answer, "No, it was I who found you."

Acts 15:22–31
Psalm 57:8–9,10 and 12
John 15:12–17

Saturday

MAY 20

• ST. BERNARDINE OF SIENA, PRIEST •

Day after day the churches grew stronger in faith and increased
in number.
—ACTS 16:5–6

We've been following Paul on his journeys. The names of the
ancient cities become a beautiful list: Antioch, Seleucia,
Cyprus, Salamis, and Paphos; Perga, Pisidia, Iconium, Derbe,
and Lystra. And today it's the regions of Phrygia, Galatia,
Mysia, and Troas. We don't have a litany of cities the way we
have the Litany of the Saints, but I think I would like such a
song. In one long recital we'd recall those distant places,
most of which are no longer there but whose dust and graves
still lie beneath the current layer of ground. We'd trace a map
beneath our present map and remember that long walk that
built our church.

Acts 16:1–10
Psalm 100:1b–2,3,5
John 15:18–21

⇒ 175 ⇐

Sunday

MAY 21

Always be ready to give an explanation to anyone who asks you for a reason for your hope, but do it with gentleness and reverence, keeping your conscience clear.
—1 PETER 3:15–16

The first summer I was home from college, I had lunch with an old friend. We discussed death as college students tend to do. "I think we just dissolve into the earth," she said. "And I like that idea, of my body turning into flowers and trees." I was openly appalled. But if I'd said to her, "Jesus Christ is my hope," my words would have had less meaning to her than flowers did to me. We can't assume our words will translate, so we must speak with gentleness and reverence and keep our conscience clear. After all, the very flowers that she imagined becoming might someday turn her eyes to God and so in fact become a reason for hope.

Acts 8:5–8,14–17
Psalm 66:1–3,4–5,6–7,16, 20 (1)
1 Peter 3:15–18
John 14:15–21

*A woman named Lydia, a dealer in purple cloth, from the city of
Thyatira, a worshiper of God, listened.*
—ACTS 16:14

Lydia takes her name from the region of Lydia, which
included her home city of Thyatira. The Thyatirians made a
dye from the madder root in an intricate process. It involved,
says Jill Goodwin in *A Dyer's Manual*, "sumac and oak galls,
calf's blood, sheep's dung, oil, soda, alum and a solution of
tin." It sounds like a witch's brew, but out of it came a deep
shade of purple. Some say it rivaled the purple from Tyre,
made from the crushed shells of murex snails. We would have
forgotten her altogether, this Lydian lady, who made
mysterious cloth and worshiped God, if it weren't for that
particular Sabbath afternoon, when beyond the city gates
and along the river, she unknowingly became the first
European to sit and listen to Paul and Timothy and Silas
and believe.

Acts 16:11–15
Psalm 149:1b–2, 3–4, 5–6a and 9b
John 15:26–16:4a

Sirs, what must I do to be saved?
—ACTS 16:30

The jailer sat outside the prison in which the disciples lay beaten, their feet chained to stakes. He expected moans, but instead hymns came drifting through the bars. When he finally managed to doze off, an earthquake shook him awake. He gaped at the ruined jail, doors thrown open and chains loose. He'd be killed for letting them go, but maybe tortured first. So he raised his sword to kill himself, and someone cried, "Do no harm!" He dropped his sword and fell down before these stripped and bleeding men. "Sirs," he gasped, "what must I do to be saved?" He couldn't have meant saved from death, for the authorities would still want his head. He meant saved like they were saved. Saved so rather than raise his sword in the face of death he might sing.

Acts 16:22–34
Psalm 138:1–2ab,2cde–3,7c–8
John 16:5–11

I even discovered an altar inscribed, "To an Unknown God."
—ACTS 17:23

Paul is struck by how close the Athenians have gotten to the truth. "What therefore you unknowingly worship," he says, "I proclaim to you. . . . [H]e who gives to everyone life and breath and everything." And God does all this, Paul goes on, "so that people might seek God, even perhaps grope for him and find him, though indeed he is not far from any one of us." And then as if to show them how close they are, he quotes Epimenides, one of the Athenians' own poets: "For 'in him we live and move and have our being.'" I love that this line, like an original creed, stands at the center of our liturgy. So often we are still like them. We still grope for this hidden God—not far from any one of us, closer than breath or bone—and sometimes find him.

Acts 17:15,22–18:1
Psalm 148:1–2,11–12,13,14
John 16:12–15

Thursday

MAY 25

• THE ASCENSION OF THE LORD • ST. BEDE THE VENERABLE, PRIEST AND
DOCTOR OF THE CHURCH • ST. GREGORY VII, POPE
• ST. MARY MAGDALENE DE' PAZZI, VIRGIN •

What is this "little while" of which he speaks?
—JOHN 16:18

The phrase "little while" occurs seven times in this passage
for today. "A little while and you will no longer see me," says
Jesus, "and again a little while later and you will see me." A
little while and the stars will cool and the planets turn to
rock. A little while and a bird will sing and the sun slip down
beneath the horizon. In God's time, a little while could be an
eon or a blink. "What is this 'little while' of which he speaks?"
the disciples ask. One little while is our lives. And in this
little while, as Jesus says today, we will surely grieve and
mourn, but not too long later, our grief will become joy.

EASTER WEEKDAY:
Acts 18:1–8
Psalm 98:1,2–3ab,3cd–4
John 16:16–20

THE ASCENSION OF THE LORD:
Acts 1:1–11
Psalm 47:2–3,6–7,8–9(6)
Ephesians 1:17–23
Matthew 28:16–20

Friday

MAY 26

• ST. PHILIP NERI, PRIEST •

I will see you again, and your hearts will rejoice, and no one will take your joy away from you. On that day you will not question me about anything.

—JOHN 16:22

In today's reading Jesus has just told the disciples, "You will no longer see me." They are in anguish and full of questions, wanting to know why. There will be anguish, yes, Jesus tells them. But when it's over, a joy so complete, so final, will come and silence every question, silence it, he says, the way a newborn child erases the pain of childbirth. I remember those tremendous, ripping surges of effort, but as soon as my baby lay there breathing on my chest, I wished I could do it again. In a similar way I find myself missing Lent, longing for that sorrow, for that feeling of being closer to joy than I am in everyday life, so close we could already see the answering light cast back.

Acts 18:9–18
Psalm 47:2–3,4–5,6–7
John 16:20–23

The hour is coming when I will no longer speak to you in figures but I will tell you clearly about the Father.
—JOHN 16:25

Jesus has been trying to tell everyone who he is, but how do you explain something beyond all experience? "I am the bread of life," he said. "I am the light of the world." And since all language points beyond itself, the disciples understood him to mean, "I am *like* bread, I am *like* light." In this one case, however, the person who said these words is the Word of Life, the one Word that is the source of its own meaning, and for that matter the source of everything else, too. We understand this now only because we're on the other side of Easter. On that day Jesus didn't speak in figures, he spoke clearly. He was not *like* life but Life itself.

Acts 18:23–28
Psalm 47:2–3,8–9,10
John 16:23b–28

They said, "Men of Galilee, why are you standing there looking at the sky?"
—ACTS 1:11

Just moments before the words of this passage, the disciples had watched Jesus being lifted up and a cloud taking him into the heavens. When I first approached faith, I wanted to have an experience like that, a flash of lightning, a voice booming out of nowhere, something supernatural that would finally convince me. And the Christian community I was a part of at the time considered this a good and achievable goal, for they had all apparently had such encounters. But I wish someone had come to me and laid a hand on my shoulder and said, "Why are you looking at the sky?" God is not calling us into certainty. Even the disciples that day probably saw some fuzzy, questionable cloud they could later doubt. We are being called instead into faith—faith in a God who rose.

THE ASCENSION OF THE LORD:
Acts 1:1–11
Psalm 47:2–3,6–7,8–9 (6)
Ephesians 1:17–23
Matthew 28:16–20

SEVENTH SUNDAY OF EASTER:
Acts 1:12–14
Psalm 27,14,7–8(13)
1 Peter 4:13–16
John 17:1–11a

Now you are talking plainly.
—JOHN 16:29

"Ah, now we understand," the disciples say. "We totally get it." But Jesus says, "Do you?" It's their impending loneliness, not his, that concerns him. "Each of you will be scattered to his own home," he says. Home is usually the place that solves loneliness, but he knows that when the one you miss isn't there, home becomes a great cavern of loneliness. "Here's how I solve loneliness," he says. "I am not alone, because the Father is with me." I can just see the disciples nodding their heads, "Yes, we understand." But Jesus knows they don't and begins to pray. His prayer will eventually end like this: "May the love with which you loved me be in them and I in them." We are scattered, each to our own home. May the love of Christ be scattered with us.

Acts 19:1–8
Psalm 68:2–3ab,4–5acd,6–7ab
John 16:29–33

Now I will no longer be in the world.
—JOHN 17:11

Today is a day for farewells. Jesus says he will longer be in the world, and today Paul also says, "Now I know that none of you . . . will ever see my face again." The disciples are weeping. The people of Miletus are weeping too, throwing their arms about Paul. "You draw like cords around my heart," says the traditional Christian song "The Parting Hand." It tells of drooping minds, flowing tears, and mourning souls. But there are two things to get us through. "Duty makes me understand," says the song, "that I must take the parting hand." And then, moving beyond duty, the song cries out in hope, "On that happy, happy land, we'll no more take the parting hand." It's not clear if the parting hand ever lets go until the end. The hand we grasp in duty and hope also leads us to that distant shore.

Acts 20:17–27
Psalm 68:10–11,20–21
John 17:1–11a

Wednesday

MAY 31

• THE VISITATION OF THE BLESSED VIRGIN MARY •

When Elizabeth heard Mary's greeting, the infant leaped in her womb.
—LUKE 1:41

The mother's body stands as a physical barrier to this world.
The baby inside, curled up, oblivious, knows nothing of what
lies beyond. Mary was pregnant, and still it was just her own
body the world could see, a skirt rounding out. But this
blindness was in one direction. Inside that dim, floating
interior, Jesus saw through the layers of muscle and skin and
cloth. And his vision, so strong it came like a hand or face,
stirred the life of the one who lay hidden within Elizabeth's
body. In this moment we get a snapshot of how the story will
go: the barriers of birth and death will fall away, and Jesus
will be left there, stirring the lives of all of us who can't yet
see what lies beyond.

Zephaniah 3:14–18a or Romans 12:9–16
Isaiah 12:2–3,4bcd,5–6
Luke 1:39–56

Thursday

JUNE 1

• ST. JUSTIN, MARTYR •

I am on trial for hope in the resurrection of the dead.
—ACTS 23:6

Today Paul makes a proclamation to the Sanhedrin. And the
Sadducees declare that there is no resurrection, or for that
matter angels or spirits. But the Pharisees wonder, "Suppose a
spirit or an angel *has* spoken to him?" Their question is the
great *perhaps* of faith. Perhaps it's all true. The Jewish
philosopher Martin Buber tells a story that turns on this same
possibility. An atheist scholar comes to see a rabbi and rails
against religion, trying to prove it false. The rabbi paces back
and forth with a book in hand but suddenly stops, glances
up, and says, "But perhaps it's all true after all." It was that
terrible *perhaps*, Buber says, that finally brought the scholar to
faith. That same *perhaps* must have haunted the Sadducees
that day. It still haunts our world now. Perhaps it's all true.

Acts 22:30; 23:6–11
Psalm 16:1–2a and 5,7–8,9–10,11
John 17:20–26

Simon, son of John, do you love me?
—JOHN 21:16

The rule of three originates in ancient oral tradition. Events or ideas are more powerful, more easily remembered, when they come in threes. These sets of three show up in both fairy tales and religious tradition. There are three little pigs, three visits from a wicked stepmother, three guesses at a name. Three persons in the Trinity, three days before rising, three denials. In Latin, *omne trium perfectum* means "everything that comes in threes is perfect." Today Jesus asks three times, "Simon, son of John, do you love me?" and three times he tells Simon Peter, "Feed my sheep." He's trying to bring Peter's heart to perfection, so he lays these words—*love me, feed my sheep*—over his life three times. A cord of three strands, it says in Ecclesiastes 4:12, is not easily broken. Peter will cling to this cord all his life: as he bids Jesus farewell, builds the Church, and dies.

Acts 25:13b–21
Psalm 103:1–2,11–12,19–20ab
John 21:15–19

Saturday

JUNE 3

What concern is it of yours? You follow me.
—JOHN 21:22

It's the day before Pentecost, the close of the Gospel of John.
The disciple who testified to these things has finished his
account and the season of Easter is almost over. Everything
that will come after is about to begin. We, too, are at this
same place in the calendar. So of course just like the
disciples, we want to know what's coming. It's a matter of
providence. Theologians have written endless tomes on this
topic, but no matter how we theorize, the future remains
dark. "What concern is it of yours?" Jesus says today. "You
follow me." So we go forward into Ordinary Time, making
our way in darkness. But the way is not entirely dark, for as
the poet Gerard Manley Hopkins says, "Sometimes a lantern
moves along the night," and we follow it.

Acts 28:16–20,30–31
Psalm 11:4,5, and 7
John 21:20–25

JUNE 4

• PENTECOST SUNDAY •

*And when he had said this, he breathed on them and said to them,
"Receive the Holy Spirit."*
—JOHN 20:22

The first account of Pentecost describes a noise like driving
wind and then tongues of fire, which parted and came to rest
on each of the disciples. But in the second account Jesus says
simply, "Peace be with you," and breathes on them. What
was it like? Like wind or fire? More likely the experience was
otherworldly, and only later did the disciples reach for
images others could understand. I like to imagine that there
was no actual wind show or fireworks that day, just the
indescribable breath of God. For what we celebrate today is
not just an ancient event but something that happens again
and again. There probably won't be wind or fire, but Christ is
alive, still breathing, still sending his spirit upon us.

VIGIL:
Genesis 11:1–9 or Exodus
19:3–8a,16–20b or Ezekiel 37:1–4 or
Joel 3:1–5
Psalm 104:1–2,24,35,27–28,29,30
Romans 8:22–27
John 7:37–39

DAY:
Acts 2:1–11
Psalm 104:1,24,29–30,31,34
1 Corinthians 12:3b–7,12–13
John 20:19–23

Monday

JUNE 5

• ST. BONIFACE, BISHOP AND MARTYR •

I, Tobit, have lived all the days of my life on the paths of truth and righteousness.
—TOBIT 1:3

Tobit reads like a religious novel, written in first-person and full of detail. Today Tobit sends his son to find a poor man with whom they might dine. When his son reports instead that he found their kinsman strangled in the marketplace, Tobit springs to his feet, leaves his dinner untouched, and carries in the dead man. Later Tobit eats in sorrow, remembering the prophecy, "Your festivals shall be turned into mourning, / and all your songs into lamentation," and he weeps. We are drawn into the story. We, too, have wept over food, imagined doom, and wondered how we might go on. All the best novels, says author Julia Glass, are about this same thing: how we go on. So all week we'll read Tobit's story to find out how one man does this.

Tobit 1:3; 2:1b–8
Psalm 112:1b–2,3b–4,5–6
Mark 12:1–12

Tuesday

JUNE 6

• ST. NORBERT, BISHOP •

Jesus said to them, "Repay to Caesar what belongs to Caesar and to
God what belongs to God."
—MARK 12:17

Some people believe religion must be political. Others
believe our politics must be religious. But Jesus is treading a
fine, difficult line between these two positions. He is saying
that we do have obligations in both the political and
religious spheres, but we must figure out which belong to
which. This is not an easy task. In the opening lines of
Romans 13, Paul writes about these very questions but ends
by saying, "Owe nothing to anyone, except to love one
another." When the task of sorting out the political and the
religious, the social and the intimate, the world and the
home, becomes too great, remember in the end it is only love
we owe to one another.

Tobit 2:9–14
Psalm 112:1–2,7–8,9
Mark 12:13–17

At that very time, the prayer of these two suppliants was heard.
—TOBIT 3:16

As we live, life can seem random. Yet if we focus in on a single moment once it's past, and spin out the history of this moment in all directions, how everyone traveled to this place and time, it can seem preordained. Tobit in Ninevah wanted to die. Far away in Media his cousin Sarah did too. So when their unrelated lives suddenly converged in a surprising and redemptive way, it seemed fated. And according to Tobit's account, it was. At the very time they separately prayed to die, their prayers were heard in heaven. The angel Raphael was dispatched and came, disguised, to set things right. Life may appear random as we go, but eventually we'll see how providence traveled with us like an angel on foot.

Tobit 3:1–11a,16–17a
Psalm 25:2–3,4–5ab,6 and 7bc,8–9
Mark 12:18–27

Thursday

JUNE 8

[God] is One and there is no other.
—MARK 12:32

I've been reading an introduction to the Sanskrit *Vedas*, an ancient sacred collection of texts, which describes early religious sentiment: "We see man watching the outside world with joy and wonder. He watches the beauty of the dawn and the glory of the sun and . . . loves this beautiful creation and feels that his love cannot but be answered by a great love." We don't have to give up on our creed to recognize this as a true religious experience. For God is One, and there is no other. No nation, building, theory, or person can hold God in one place. So of course, in the warmth of the rising sun, these ancient people already felt that great love, which we Christians refer to as Christ, and reached out for it.

Tobit 6:10–11; 7:1bcde,9–17; 8:4–9a
Psalm 128:1–2,3,4–5
Mark 12:28–34

"Now that I have seen you again, son, I am ready to die!"
And she sobbed aloud.
—TOBIT 11:9

The death of a child is always too soon. We are not meant to
be standing there looking at our child's fresh grave. It
provides the odd sensation of being too old already, seeing
things we were never meant to see. For weeks Anna thought
her son Tobiah was dead. "I want to be where he is," she must
have thought, longing to collapse time and space and find at
least his body. "It should have been me," she must have
prayed. So when she saw him coming down the road, she
ran, hysterical, and touched his hair and feet. Right then, she
must have wished she could lay her life down for him. "I am
ready to die!" she said. And she was, for as it says in Matthew,
whoever loses his life shall find it.

Tobit 11:5–17
Psalm 146:1b–2,6c–7,8–9a,9bc–10
Mark 12:35–37

JUNE 10

I am Raphael, one of the seven angels who enter and serve before the
Glory of the Lord.
—TOBIT 12:15

"Where are the days of Tobias," writes Rilke about the book
of Tobit, "when one of you, veiling his radiance, stood at the
front door, slightly disguised for the journey, no longer
appalling?" Tobit's encounter with the angel began that way.
Raphael showed up looking like any other man. But later he
revealed himself, and stricken with fear, Tobit and his son fell
to the ground. "If the archangel now, perilous, from behind
the stars took even one step down toward us," writes Rilke,
"our own heart, beating higher and higher would beat us to
death." The novel *Tobit* gives us the portrait of an angel:
gentle, walking by our side, and then radiant, perilous, from
behind the stars. We should recall what the psalms say: God
has commanded angels such as these to guard us wherever
we go.

Tobit 12:1,5–15,20
Tobit 13:2,6efgh,7,8
Mark 12:38–44

Sunday

JUNE 11

• THE MOST HOLY TRINITY •

*The grace of the Lord Jesus Christ and the love of God and the fellowship
of the Holy Spirit be with all of you.*
—2 CORINTHIANS 13:13

Every Mass begins with the Trinitarian blessing in today's
passage. We automatically respond, often without thinking,
"And with your spirit." Until now, I didn't realize these were
Paul's words to the Corinthians. It's beautiful to read what
comes before. "Brothers and sisters," Paul says in that
intimate way, "rejoice!" And then he urges them to encourage
and agree with one another. "Live in peace," he says, "and the
God of love and peace will be with you." To read this here, in
a letter that once traveled from Paul's hands into the hands of
a particular person, brings it to life for me. In Mass today,
hear these words not as the recitation of a script but as an
intimate and urgent message, a letter addressed to you.

Exodus 34:4b–6,8–9
Daniel 3:52,53,54,55, (52b)
2 Corinthians 13:11–13
John 3:16–18

Look to him that you may be radiant with joy,
and your faces may not blush with shame.
—PSALM 34:6

This past year I have seen a number of older female singers in concert: Rory Block, Rickie Lee Jones, Iris DeMent. Each one had a confidence that seems reserved for people over 50. Rory Block forgot lines and laughed and started over. Rickie Lee Jones changed her shoes on stage, switching from platform heels to neon pink sneakers. "When left to our own devices," she said, "singers wear shocking colors." Iris DeMent borrowed lipstick from someone in the audience and put it on in front of everyone. But even more, when they sang, their faces were radiant, their voices huge. I watched them and thought that this is what we all want, to get outside of ourselves, let our spirits scream out our songs, and not blush for shame.

2 Corinthians 1:1–7
Psalm 34:2–3,4–5,6–7,8–9
Matthew 5:1–12

Tuesday

JUNE 13

Your light must shine before others.
—MATTHEW 5:16

Today Jesus gives us three disparate images: You are salt of
the earth. A city set on a mountain cannot be hidden. A lamp
is not put under a bushel basket. It reads like a riddle—what
is at once like salt, a city on a hill, and a lamp? A lamp *should
not* be hidden but should be allowed to light the house. A
city on a hill *cannot* be hidden. And salt, that one crucial
ingredient, *is* hidden, worked into food and dispersed. So
what, then, should not be hidden, cannot be hidden, but is
also the one vital, hidden thing? It is the light of Christ,
which lies dispersed inside each of us and which we should
not hide. And thank God we hold this light together, like a
city, for never will every single light in every single house
go out.

2 Corinthians 1:18–22
Psalm 119:129,130,131,132,133,135
Matthew 5:13–16

*For if what was going to fade was glorious, how much more will what
endures be glorious.*
—2 CORINTHIANS 3:11

I just finished reading the novel *All the Light We Cannot See*, by
Anthony Doerr. At one point a blind girl asks her caretaker,
"Do you think, Madame, that in heaven we will really get to
see God face-to-face?" "We might," Madame answers. "But
what if you're blind?" says the girl. "I'd expect that if God
wants us to see something," Madame says, "we'll see it." They
are lying in a field of weeds, which sway and shimmy,
listening to the bees and hoverflies, writes Doerr. And
Madame says, "Now that I think about it, child, I expect
heaven is a lot like this." If it's a lot like this, which will fade,
how much more will what endures be glorious? And what
God wants us to see, blind as we are, we'll see.

2 Corinthians 3:4–11
Psalm 99:5,6,7,8,9
Matthew 5:17–19

Thursday

JUNE 15

The Lord is the Spirit and where the Spirit of the Lord is, there is freedom.
—2 CORINTHIANS 3:17

People wrongly imagine that freedom means freedom from
all rules and commandments. Nothing could be farther from
the truth. Freedom comes only by fusing our own will with
that great Will. The poet Walt Whitman calls this great Will
the universal, eternal laws, which he says run "through all
Time, pervade history, prove immortality, give moral purpose
to the entire objective world, and the last dignity to
human life."

2 Corinthians 3:15–4:1,3–6
Psalm 85:9ab and 10,11–12,13–14
Matthew 5:20–26

⇒ 201 ⇐

Death is at work in us, but life in you.
—2 CORINTHIANS 4:12

Recently a local college girl jumped off the top of a parking garage to her death. In a farewell note she said the suicide of a student athlete at the University of Pennsylvania had shown her the way. She knew about this other story only because ESPN had covered the event in lyric detail. "She had wings on," they wrote. And later: "Maybe she could only imagine the freedom of flying." It gave suicide a romantic, glossy feel. And the Penn student, in turn, had said that it was social media that broke her, those endless, edited snapshots of other people's perfect lives. Life on Instagram. Death in the news. How different from the experience of a flesh-and-blood community in which tragedy and triumph interweave. There are no glossy shots, just real people, walking up the aisle in hope, with their canes and their babies, their joys and trials and unfiltered faces.

2 Corinthians 4:7–15
Psalm 116:10–11,15–16,17–18
Matthew 5:27–32

Saturday

JUNE 17

Let your "Yes" mean "Yes," and your "No" mean "No."
—MATTHEW 5:37

We often imagine that not wavering between yes and no is a matter of knowing what we want. I'm reminded of a scene in the movie *Runaway Bride*. "You're so lost, you don't even know what kind of eggs you like!" says Richard Gere. "*What?*" says Julia Roberts. "That's right. With the priest, you wanted scrambled. With the Deadhead, it was fried. With the bug guy, it was poached. And now it's egg whites only." "That's called changing your mind," says Roberts. "No, that's called not having a mind of your own," says Gere. We imagine that buried inside each of us is "a mind of our own" with clear preferences about eggs and hairstyles and vacations. But today Jesus is urging us to be like our Father in heaven. We won't find singleness of purpose on our own—we'll find it by following Another.

2 Corinthians 5:14–21
Psalm 103:1–2,3–4,9–10,11–12
Matthew 5:33–37

⇒ 203 ⇐

Sunday

JUNE 18

• THE MOST HOLY BODY AND BLOOD OF CHRIST (CORPUS CHRISTI) •

For my flesh is true food, and my blood is true drink.
—JOHN 6:55

Sailors talk about true wind and apparent wind. Apparent wind is what sailors experience blowing on their sails and face as they move across the water. It is also what we experience as we walk on a windy day. But really this wind is the combined effects of our own movements and true wind. True wind is the actual air that blows across land or water, unencumbered. We can't experience true wind, because as soon as we sail or step into it we've changed it. In the same way, true food and true drink remain mysterious to us, but we can step up to the altar and receive them. And although we don't change this food and drink, they change us. And what we think of as ourselves, that exterior, apparent thing, begins to fall away and we become more our true selves.

Deuteronomy 8:2–3,14b–16a
Psalm 147:12–13,14–15,19–20 (12)
1 Corinthians 10:16–17
John 6:51–58

———————

∋204∈

Monday

JUNE 19

• ST. ROMUALD, ABBOT •

Behold, now is a very acceptable time;
behold, now is the day of salvation.
—2 CORINTHIANS 6:2

The philosopher Richard Taylor offers this thought experiment: A man goes for a walk in a forest and stumbles across a translucent white ball. The sky and earth he ignores, but this ball full of mystery? He circles it, wondering, and finally comes to the conclusion that only someone, some being, could have placed it there. What he doesn't notice, Taylor says, is that he could just as easily have circled any tree, any rock, and wondered at its existence. As we get older our capacity for wonder dims. The world becomes gradually predictable and ordinary. Only occasionally do we wake up and behold the utterly inexplicable givenness of the world around us and in our very lives. "We appeal to you," Paul urges today, "not to receive the grace of God in vain."

2 Corinthians 6:1–10
Psalm 98:1,2b,3ab,3cd–4
Matthew 5:38–42

⇒205⇐

*The abundance of their joy and their profound poverty overflowed in a
wealth of generosity on their part.*
—2 CORINTHIANS 8:2

Sometimes as I read the New Testament epistles, I get the
sense that the early Church, composed of scattered
communities, was makeshift and noninstitutional. But in
today's reading we get a different picture. Paul is taking up
what historians call the Jerusalem collection. He's going from
church to church, encouraging each community to give to
the larger Body of Christ. He is urging unity and love across
geographic, economic, and racial boundaries. And it's clear in
this massive, organized relief effort that the churches weren't
operating alone but as parts of a whole. For the sake of unity,
we see the Church necessarily becoming an institution,
which means a body that can function as one.

2 Corinthians 8:1–9
Psalm 146:2,5–6ab,6c–7,8–9a
Matthew 5:43–48

Wednesday

JUNE 21

• ST. ALOYSIUS GONZAGA, RELIGIOUS •

Whoever sows sparingly will also reap sparingly, and whoever sows
bountifully will also reap bountifully.
—2 CORINTHIANS 9:6

There's an old adage that goes, "Only the one who works gets bread." The philosopher Søren Kierkegaard commented that oddly enough this adage does not fit the world. And he meant the visible, external world. In this world, often those who do not work get plenty of bread while the hard laborers go hungry. But in the realm of the Spirit, the adage is not only true but also strictly and always true: only those who work get bread. Only those who hunger and thirst after righteousness will be filled. Yet it's a different kind of bread, a different kind of filling. If we work hard in the visible world, give bountifully, only sometimes will we be compensated, but inside our spirits will widen and gentle and begin to fill with an even greater bounty.

2 Corinthians 9:6–11
Psalm 112:1bc–2,3–4,9
Matthew 6:1–6,16–18

Thursday

JUNE 22

• ST. PAULINUS OF NOLA, BISHOP • ST. JOHN FISHER, BISHOP AND MARTYR, •
ST. THOMAS MORE, MARTYR •

*If only you would put up with a little foolishness from me! Please put up
with me.*
—2 CORINTHIANS 11:1

It's hard to determine St. Paul's tone in this passage. "I am
talking like an insane person!" he continues later
(2 Corinthians 11:23 NAB). I like to imagine he was smiling as
he spoke, chiding the Corinthians for accepting false
teaching. Today is the feast day of St. Thomas More, who,
like Paul, stood against the fragmentation of the Church.
Also like St. Paul, More was an imposing legal figure. But he
was known, as Erasmus reports, for being "always expressive
of an amiable joyousness, and even an incipient laughter." In
the film *A Man for All Seasons*, More's final words are that
God "will not refuse one who is so blithe to go to him." And
blithe, I think, is the right word for Paul's tone. St. Paul and
St. Thomas More were both blithe in the face of trial.

2 Corinthians 11:1–11
Psalm 111:1b–2,3–4,7–8
Matthew 6:7–15

Friday

JUNE 23

• THE MOST SACRED HEART OF JESUS •

The LORD set his heart on you.
—DEUTERONOMY 7:6

The image of the Sacred Heart is shaped like a vase with smoke or flames sprouting from its neck. Sometimes it floats freely with wings. Sometimes Christ holds it in his hand as if he could actually set his heart somewhere else. "Who is there who would not love this wounded heart?" asks St. Bonaventure. "Who would not love in return Him, who loves so much?" Today we meditate on the source of love. "And this is love," says St. John today, "not that we have loved God, but that he loved us." The image of the sacred heart is everywhere, on big-armed tattoos, in rickshaws in India, in gilded icons. But if you find the image too gaudy or strange, close your eyes and meditate instead on your own heart, which beats with the great love that moves the tides and is set on you.

Deuteronomy 7:6–11
Psalm 103:1–2,3–4,6–7,8,10 (see 17)
1 John 4:7–16
Matthew 11:25–30

———————

*[The prophets] were serving not themselves but you with regard to the
things . . . into which angels longed to look.*
—1 PETER 1:12

Imagine the days of the calendar as a circle. Mark Christmas at
the top with a tiny star and mentally extend a line from that
star to every other day on the circle. It will look like light
streaming from a single point. We're standing at midsummer,
on a feast that is often called Summer Christmas, directly
across the circle from the star. So close to the solstice, we take
in more light than any at other time of the year. I picture
Elizabeth and John forever standing at this midpoint, arms
open, as if to enclose a small bit of the circle and hold the light
that pours down. "Make ready the way of the Lord," cries John.

"Blessed are you who believed," cries Elizabeth
(Luke 1:45 NAB). And now we stand with them and gaze across
at that moment into which angels longed to look.

VIGIL:
Jeremiah 1:4–10
Psalm 71:1–2,3–4a,5–6ab,15ab and 17
1 Peter 1:8–12
Luke 1:5–17

DAY:
Isaiah 49:1–6
Psalm 139:1b–3,13–14ab,14c–15
Acts 13:22–26
Luke 1:57–66,80

Death reigned from Adam to Moses, even over those who did not sin after the pattern of the trespass of Adam, who is the type of the one who was to come.

—ROMANS 5:14

Here we have two images: Adam's trespass and Adam himself. His trespass becomes the pattern for death, the original from which copies can be made. And though we like to think of ourselves as individuals, in this regard we are all cut from this same mortal cloth. But then Adam himself is called the type of the one who was to come. A type is a symbol that anticipates a greater realization. So Adam gives us both the image of death and the image of Life. Salvation is that which loosens and lets fall away that first, deadly image from the second.

Jeremiah 20:10–13
Psalm 69:8–10,14,17,33–35 (14c)
Romans 5:12–15
Matthew 10:26–33

Monday

JUNE 26

I will bless you;
I will make your name great,
so that you will be a blessing.
—GENESIS 12:2

There is a beautiful passage in Marilynne Robinson's novel *Gilead* when the old preacher recalls blessing kittens as a child. "I still remember how those warm little brows felt under the palm of my hand," says the preacher. "Everyone has petted a cat, but to touch one like that, with the pure intention of blessing it, is a very different thing. It stays in the mind. For years we would wonder what, from a cosmic viewpoint, we had done to them." He goes on to say that there's a reality in blessing, the sensation of really knowing a creature. We may not feel it, that hand on our brow, that pure intention, but it's there always, knowing us and changing who we are.

Genesis 12:1–9
Psalm 33:12–13,18–19,20 and 22
Matthew 7:1–5

Tuesday

JUNE 27

Let there be no strife between you and me.
—GENESIS 13:8

"Do not . . . throw your pearls before swine," Jesus says today, but also, "Do to others whatever you would have them do to you." It's a quandary: how to be at once guarded and ever loving. Today we see Abram manage it. There's strife between his people and Lot's, so Abram says, "Please separate from me. If you prefer the left, I will go to the right. If you prefer the right, I will go to the left." He is kind but clear. Similarly, the psychologist Henry Cloud wrote, "Boundaries define what is me and what is not me. . . . A boundary shows me where I end and someone else begins." Before you can practice the Golden Rule, you need to know what is you and what is not you. You need to be able, as Abram did, to draw a line in the sand.

Genesis 13:2,5–18
Psalm 15:2–3a,3bc–4ab,5
Matthew 7:6,12–14

⇒ 213 ⇐

Wednesday

JUNE 28

• ST. IRENAEUS, BISHOP AND MARTYR •

It was on that occasion that the LORD made a covenant with Abram.
—GENESIS 15:18

I'm not sure what I expected a covenant to look like—maybe
not an angel and a sober saint bent over a desk—but surely
not this bloody scene: a heifer, a she-goat, and a ram laid out
in raw halves, as if they could be folded back together again;
birds of prey mantling over the carcasses while Abram keeps
watch; and coming into this terrifying dark, a smoking fire
pot and flaming torch. But why are we, who know of disease
and genocide and famine, so shocked? If God dares make a
covenant here, wouldn't he have to come like this, into our
destruction and gore, and show us he could actually do it,
fold us back together again and make us whole? And isn't the
cross exactly that, a torch shining in the terrifying dark?

Genesis 15:1–12,17–18
Psalm 105:1–2,3–4,6–7,8–9
Matthew 7:15–20

⇒ 214 ⇐

Thursday

JUNE 29

• SS. PETER AND PAUL, APOSTLES •

Day pours out the word to day;
and night to night imparts knowledge.
—PSALM 19:2

There are two kinds of revelation, general and special. General revelation is what we can discern by observation. We study the world, listening to the chattering skies, which the psalm describes as pouring out the Word, and we learn something of the universe and God. But it's never enough, and we're left longing for more. Special revelation takes us beyond what we could have figured out on our own. We receive hints, images, possibilities from nature and history, but only when a sentence like Peter's "You are the Christ, the Son of the living God" breaks into our consciousness are we able to truly understand what nature has been trying to say all along. Today we give thanks for St. Peter and St. Paul, who received and passed on a message we never could have guessed.

VIGIL:
Acts 3:1–10
Psalm 19:2–3,4–5
Galatians 1:11–20
John 21:15–19

DAY:
Acts 12:1–11
Psalm 34:2–3,4–5,6–7,8–9
2 Timothy 4:6–8,17–18
Matthew 16:13–19

I am God the Almighty. Walk in my presence and be blameless.
—GENESIS 17:1

It must be incredible to see a city burn. "It was like a snowstorm only the flakes were red instead of white," wrote Bessie Bradwell Helmer in her memoir about the Great Chicago Fire. In AD 64 fire razed the city of Rome. Nero cruelly accused Christians of "firing the city," wrote Tacitus, who then gave this grim account: "Covered with the skins of beasts, they were torn by dogs and perished, or were nailed to crosses, or were doomed to the flames and burnt, to serve as a nightly illumination." Peter and Paul were likely among those killed. Rome looked on as these first martyrs burned, people who had walked in God's presence and had been blameless. As a result, "there arose a feeling of compassion," according to Tacitus. And that compassion, born of all that burning, grew until it eventually converted Rome.

Genesis 17:1,9–10,15–22
Psalm 137:1–2,3,4–5, 6
Matthew 8:1–4

Saturday

JULY 1

• BLESSED JUNÍPERO SERRA, PRIEST •

Sarah laughed to herself.
—GENESIS 18:12

Today God appears as three travelers. At first you think the travelers are angels, but the passage calls them "the Lord." So there in the midday heat and dust stands the Trinity. One of them says to Abraham, "When we return, Sarah will have a son." Sarah overhears and laughs. Long ago she'd accepted the heartbreak of no children and let her life grow around that fact. So her laugh is bitter. But—she can't help it—what if it's true? So her laugh is also hopeful. "Why did Sarah laugh?" comes the voice from outside the tent. "I didn't laugh," says Sarah, trying to push her bitterness and hope back inside. "Yes you did," says the voice. Some read this as a rebuke, but to me it sounds gentle, as gentle as the Trinity appearing like common travelers at noon to convince an old woman of good news.

Genesis 18:1–15
Luke 1:46–47,48–49,50 and 53,54–55
Matthew 8:5–17

Blessed the people who know the joyful shout.
—PSALM 89:16

In *A Hole Is to Dig* and *Open House for Butterflies* writer Ruth Krauss and illustrator Maurice Sendak offer beautiful definitions and pieces of advice from a child's perspective. Here are several: "A face is something to have on the front of your head." "A floor is so you don't fall into the hole your house is in." "Yesterday shows another day is here." "A good thing to know is what a punch in the nose feels like, in case someone asks, 'Do you want a punch in the nose?'" But my favorite is this: "A screaming song is good to know in case you need to scream." And today, we might add, a joyful shout is good to know in case you feel joyful.

2 Kings 4:8–11,14–16a
Psalm 89:2–3,16–17,18–19 (2a)
Romans 6:3–4, 8–11
Matthew 10:37–42

Monday

JULY 3

• ST. THOMAS, APOSTLE •

*You are no longer strangers and sojourners, but you are fellow citizens
with the holy ones and members of the household of God.*
—EPHESIANS 2:19

It's generally considered foolish to believe anything without
evidence. Doubting Thomas remained skeptical until he
touched the very wounds of Christ. But today those wounds
that once counted as evidence can be chalked up to a dream.
For how do we know what Thomas actually saw? Where is
our proof? However, this quest for hard evidence
misunderstands the nature of belief. "If you do not believe,"
says Martin Luther, "then you do not abide." Paul's letter to
the Ephesians explains it like this: You begin as sojourners
searching for something out there. You are ungrounded,
homeless. Only belief allows you to stop being a stranger
and abide in a household. "Blessed are those who have not
seen and have believed," Jesus tells Thomas, for he knows
even for Thomas it's the only way.

Ephesians 2:19–22
Psalm 117:1bc,2
John 20:24–29

God destroyed the Cities of the Plain.
—GENESIS 19:29

Lot escapes outside the city gates but is still in danger. "Get off to the hills!" people warn. But there's not enough time, so he heads for a nearby town. "It's only a small place," he cries, praying for it to be spared. It's easy to look back on battles won and great escapes and see them as inevitable victories, as if the sure hand of providence was clearly there all along. But on the ground, in the midst of possible destruction, it never feels like that. On the ground, reliance on providence is always an act of courage. Our Declaration of Independence, signed with no victory in sight, ends like this: "For the support of this Declaration, with a firm reliance on the protection of divine providence, we mutually pledge to each other our Lives, our Fortunes and our sacred Honor."

Genesis 19:15–29
Psalm 26:2–3,9–10,11–12
Matthew 8:23–27

• ST. ANTHONY ZACCARIA, PRIEST • ST. ELIZABETH OF PORTUGAL •

God heard the boy's cry.
—GENESIS 21:17

Far before the Resurrection of Jesus, the Old Testament hints at resurrection. Prompted by a domestic dispute with Sarah, Abraham sends Hagar and their young child Ishmael into the desert. When the skin of water runs dry, Hagar falls into despair. She sets her tiny son down under a shrub and goes a good distance away. We can see them now as if from above, parched and dying under their separate shrubs, the well of Beersheba just paces away. But God hears the boy cry, and through his angel says, "Arise." It whispers to us of what's coming, the *talitha koum* of the New Testament (see January 31). "Arise, lift up the boy," says the angel and leads them to the well. If only we could look at our own lives from above and see that well that is just paces away and hear the voice calling us to arise.

Genesis 21:5,8–20a
Psalm 34:7–8,10–11,12–13
Matthew 8:28–34

Our God is in heaven;
whatever he wills, he does.
Their idols are silver and gold,
the handiwork of men.
—PSALM 115:3

If we make our own god, like the pagans do in today's psalm, then there's no help for us. We cannot create that which saves us. It would be like that absurd attempt by the fictional character Baron Munchausen to pull himself out of the bog by his own hair. Or it would be like that old joke about the earth riding on the back of a turtle. When the obvious question comes, "But what is the turtle standing on?" the punch line is, "It's turtles all the way down." Again, it's funny but absurd, for there must be a final ground on which everything rests. We cannot lift ourselves up, we cannot be that which supports the whole. We must trust in something that is truly beyond us or we have no trust at all.

Genesis 22:1b–19
Psalm 115:1–2,3–4,5–6,8–9
Matthew 9:1–8

In his love for her, Isaac found solace after the death of his mother Sarah.
—GENESIS 24:67

I recently watched *The Better Angels*, a film about the boyhood of Abraham Lincoln. It begins with Lincoln's statement, "All that I am, or hope to be, I owe to my angel mother." Lincoln's mother died when he was only nine years old. Another woman raised him, gave him the books that shaped him, and even said, "His mind and mine seem to run together." And yet he never forgot his angel mother. When a person dies, we can find solace in other loves. We can form new loves entirely. But that prior love is never subsumed, never replaced, for the nature of love is eternity.

Genesis 23:1–4,19; 24:1–8,62–67
Psalm 106:1b–2,3–4a,4b–5
Matthew 9:9–13

All that the LORD wills he does,
in heaven and on earth,
in the seas and in all the deeps.
—PSALM 135:6

In Kate DiCamillo's children's novel *The Tale of Despereaux*, she refers to a dungeon as the "deep downs." But even in the darkness of the dungeon there is light. In the story, a little rat named Roscuro sees light for the first time in a struck match. "[The light] exploded around him," writes DiCamillo, "and danced inside him." He comes to feel that light is the only thing that matters. But later, in a fatal episode involving a chandelier and a banquet of soup, Roscuro is forced back into the deep downs and grows bitter. And yet, at a crucial moment, the smell of soup crashes "through his soul like a great wave, bringing with it the memory of light, the music, the laughter, the chandelier, everything." The Lord, the light, is there, even in all the deep downs.

Genesis 27:1–5,15–29
Psalm 135:1b–2,3–4,5–6
Matthew 9:14–17

Come to me, all you who labor and are burdened, and I will give you rest.
—MATTHEW 11:28

Whenever we have an anointing of the sick in my parish, most of the congregation comes forward. Some say this is an abuse of the sacrament, but it's hard for me to believe that God wouldn't call us forward himself, for everyone is in need of healing. It often reminds me of a line from the movie _Eve's Bayou_. One of the main characters, Mozelle Batiste Delacroix, says at one point, "All I know is most people's lives are a great disappointment to them and no one leaves this earth without feeling terrible pain. And if there is no divine explanation at the end of it all, well . . . that's sad." So we line up at the altar for ashes, for anointings, for communion—for every one of us wants an explanation. Every one of us is in need of rest.

Zechariah 9:9–10
Psalm 145:1–2,8–9,10–11,13–14 (see 1)
Romans 8:9,11–13
Matthew 11:25–30

This is nothing else but an abode of God.
—GENESIS 28:17

With a stone for a pillow, a stone that would later mark the
sacred spot, Jacob dreamed of a stairway that stretched up
from earth to heaven. And when he woke he cried out,
"Truly, the LORD is in this spot!" As a child I never knew the
biblical story of Jacob's ladder; I only learned the string trick.
Looping and dropping string from your ten fingers, you first
make cat's whiskers and then Jacob's ladder. I used to do it
with my sister's hair in the backseat of our car, her head on
my lap as I combed and chatted. I remember that little abode
between us as if it were as dear as God's own home. I look
back now and think, *Truly the Lord was in that spot, and I wish I
had a stone to mark it.*

Genesis 28:10–22a
Psalm 91:1–2,3–4,14–15ab
Matthew 9:18–26

Some man wrestled with him until the break of dawn.
—GENESIS 32:24

At first Jacob had no idea who jumped him, so he fought fiercely. But later, he began to feel a new vigor, a desire to be caught up in all that strange strength and tenderness. In Rembrandt's depiction, Jacob's face is twisted with effort, but the angel holds him as if he were a child. Jacob needed something that night, though he didn't know what, so he fought harder. "Let me go, for it is daybreak," the strange man finally said, stepping back. And only then did Jacob see him, so glorious he could hardly bear to look. "I will not let you go until you bless me," Jacob said. So often we wait for God as if it's a passive matter, but what if instead we took him on, fought him with all our strength and demanded a blessing?

Genesis 32:23–33
Psalm 17:1b,2–3,6–7ab,8b and 15
Matthew 9:32–38

We saw the anguish of his heart when he pleaded with us, yet we paid no heed.
—GENESIS 42:21

In his autobiography *The Seven Storey Mountain*, Thomas Merton recounts an episode from his boyhood. In a clump of sumac trees, Merton and his friends were building a hut with boards and tar paper and shingles. His brother, John Paul, only five years old at the time, stood a good distance away, his arms down at his sides, "offended and tremendously sad." They shouted at him to get out of there, to beat it, says Merton. They winged rocks at him but he did not move. That image of his brother's face haunted Merton for years. He calls this "terrible situation" the pattern and prototype of all sin. We separate ourselves from love, he says, "simply because it does not please us to be loved." Lord, we have callous hearts. Help us to pay heed when love is given.

Genesis 41:55–57; 42:5–7a,17–24a
Psalm 33:2–3,10–11,18–19
Matthew 10:1–7

Thursday

JULY 13

• ST. HENRY •

As you enter a house, wish it peace.
—MATTHEW 10:13

I remember a story I once read about Mother Teresa or possibly some other great saint, how she would pass people in the street and trace a little cross in her palm to bless them. I also think sometimes of the Pittsburgh nuns I once stayed with; they prayed day and night and never left their cloister. I still find myself hoping that one of those old women thinks of me as she goes on to the next bead on her rosary. And how many times has someone asked for my prayers—a friend, a priest, a little old monk at Gethsemani? Did I remember? I don't know why I find it so hard, just a cross in my palm, a single bead, a wish of peace as I pass through a door.

Genesis 44:18–21,23b–29; 45:1–5
Psalm 105:16–17,18–19,20–21
Matthew 10:7–15

—

⇒ 229 ⇐

Friday

JULY 14

• ST. KATERI TEKAKWITHA, VIRGIN •

Whoever endures to the end will be saved.
—MATTHEW 10:22

I've never understood the practice of self-mortification, all that deliberate scourging and starving. But something in the story of St. Kateri, whom we celebrate today, helped me. Her Mohawk tribe named her *Tekakwitha*, which means "she who bumps into things." Raised in a longhouse, she learned to weave from reeds and grasses. Her life was filled with terror. Smallpox ravaged her village and her face. French trappers drove her tribe into the cold forests. Mohicans launched a vicious attack on her people, and she watched prisoners of war endure torture for days. So when she converted, she must have seen the problem—a God of love and a world of horror—but also the solution: a God who fills the torture of the cross with love. So to prove such a thing was possible she would do it too, endure the worst with love.

Genesis 46:1–7,28–30
Psalm 37:3–4,18–19,27–28,39–40
Matthew 10:16–23

Saturday

JULY 15

• ST. BONAVENTURE, BISHOP AND DOCTOR OF THE CHURCH •

Are not two sparrows sold for a small coin? Yet not one of them falls to the ground without your Father's knowledge.
—MATTHEW 10:29

"I never saw a wild thing sorry for itself," writes D. H. Lawrence. "A small bird will drop frozen dead from a bough without ever having felt sorry for itself." This makes me think of when my dog got sick. "Dogs are so stoic you'll never know when they're in pain. You have to look for signs," our vet told me. "They hang their heads when they hurt." Now all the time I see old dogs faithfully staggering along on their leashes, heads held low. We can write their courage off as instinct, but I don't think that's quite right. The humblest often demonstrate the greatest nobility, and we, who are prone to self-pity, would do well to pay attention.

Genesis 49:29–32; 50:15–26a
Psalm 105:1–2,3–4,6–7
Matthew 10:24–33

*The fields are garmented with flocks
and the valleys blanketed with grain.*
—PSALM 65:14

The image in this passage speaks to me more than it might to
some, for I grew up in central Pennsylvania, where the hills
were indeed garmented with flocks and the valleys blanketed
with grain. I've seen other, more stunning landscapes, but if I
could live anywhere in the world I would go back there. It
was in those valleys I was first loved, my parents cherishing
me like God might, and it was in looking out upon those
fields that I first wondered if love itself came from
somewhere beyond our little house. There's a poem I've
always remembered by a young child: "Every day I think
about / the god and the weeds / outside and sometimes / I
hold my doll." Wherever you first thought about God and
weeds and love is likely where your rich soil lies.

Isaiah 55:10–11
Psalm 65:10,11,12–13,14
Romans 8:18–23
Matthew 13:1–23 or 13:1–9

*We were rescued like a bird
from the fowlers' snare.*
—PSALM 124:7

As on Saturday, there's talk again today of birds and pity.
Now it's not self-pity but the kind of pity that reaches out
toward others. Exodus tells of "the whole cruel fate of slaves,"
the psalm writes of birds in snares, and Jesus praises those
who give "only a cup of cold water to one of these little
ones." It's easy to be overwhelmed by the world's misery, the
torrent of waters, says the psalm, and be stunned into
inaction. The essayist Loren Eiseley, feeling stunned himself,
once met a man flinging half-dead starfish back into the sea
and marveled that the man continued on, even though that
beach, and every beach for that matter, was littered with
bodies. But Eiseley eventually found hope in this hurler of
stars, this Christ figure, "who walks, because he chooses,
always in desolation, but not in defeat."

Exodus 1:8–14,22
Psalm 124:1b–3,4–6,7–8
Matthew 10:34–11:1

I drew him out of the water.
—EXODUS 2:10

Recently, a woman in our parish lost a baby to stillbirth, as I did. She named her son Moses, she told me, because "it means drawn up from water." Reading Exodus today, I thought about how perfect that name really is. The image of the Levite woman laying her tiny son in the bulrush basket so closely mirrors what a mother must do when she buries a child. Later I came across a woodcut image of that same Old Testament moment, showing four dark angels over the lonely basket. One angel's arms are held as if cradling a child. Another gazes with the woman into her empty arms. The third appears to be pleading with heaven. And the last focuses intently on the basket. It's what I imagined during the days following my own daughter's death, dark angels around me and following my child as she drifted away.

Exodus 2:1–15a
Psalm 69:3,14,30–31,33–34
Matthew 11:20–24

Wednesday

JULY 19

There an angel of the Lord appeared to him in fire flaming out of a bush.
—EXODUS 3:2

In Orthodox theology, the burning bush is not a miracle but an actual glimpse into the uncreated energies of God. Modern cosmology talks of an original quantum flux, a "smattering of gravity-repulsive material," as one journalist put it, out of which everything exploded. All of this is disputed, of course. Western theologians don't hold with the uncreated energy theory. No scientist is sure about quantum flux. Today, curious, Moses wants to go over and "see why the bush is not burned." But instead of getting an explanation, God tells him, "Remove the sandals from your feet, for the place on which you stand is holy ground." We'll never know exactly how what preceded our world produced what we see now, but we can still remove our shoes, for surely it is holy ground.

Exodus 3:1–6,9–12
Psalm 103:1b–2,3–4,6–7
Matthew 11:25–27

"If they ask me, 'What is his name?' what am I to tell them?"
God replied, "I am who am."
—EXODUS 3:13–14

"God has a name. He is not an anonymous force," says the
Catechism of the Catholic Church, and yet "his name is at once a
name revealed and something like the refusal of a name."
When a person has a name, we can call on that name and
come to know the person who holds it. But when someone
won't tell his or her name, a great gulf opens up. Sometimes
it does feel like we are calling across a chasm, and other
times like that distance stretches inside of us to some buried
center. But the "God who reveals his name as I AM," the
Catechism goes on, "reveals himself as the God who is always
there." So even though the distance sometimes seems great,
we can call out, "God!" and believe someone is listening.

Exodus 3:13–20
Psalm 105:1 and 5,8–9,24–25,26–27
Matthew 11:28–30

• ST. LAWRENCE OF BRINDISI, PRIEST AND DOCTOR OF THE CHURCH •

Jesus was going through a field of grain on the sabbath.
—MATTHEW 12:1

I recently walked with my children through a flat field of corn in rural Illinois, only plant tips and blue sky above our heads. The stalks whispered to each other and perched on the domes of their roots, like single legs on tiptoes. It's how I picture that day: the Lord of Creation walking through the field, the corn straining on its roots to see him, whispering, "There he goes," and stretching forth its grain as an offering. The Pharisees accused Jesus and his disciples of working on the Sabbath, as if they intended a harvest rather than just plucking some ears to eat, as the Book of Deuteronomy explicitly allows. But there was no law broken that day, only an offering made by the fields to the Lord of the Sabbath as he passed by.

Exodus 11:10–12:14
Psalm 116:12–13,15 and 16bc,17–18
Matthew 12:1–8

Mary Magdalene went and announced to the disciples, "I have seen the Lord."

—JOHN 20:18

Though writer Kahlil Gibran, mixing Sufism and Christianity, is a pretty unorthodox fellow, I find his book *Jesus: The Son of Man* incredibly moving. He imagines Mary Magdalene in her scented garments and golden sandals, approaching Jesus for the first time under a cypress tree. Initially it's Jesus' comeliness, how each part of him seems to love every other part of himself, that draws her, but his eyes are her undoing. "I alone love the unseen in you," he tells her. And finally she says, "The sunset of his eyes slew the dragon in me and I became a woman, Miriam of Midjil." Through this portrait, we see Jesus as she might have, not a shining abstraction but flesh and blood. "He walked in our solitude," she says, "and visited the gardens of our passion."

Exodus 12:37–42
Psalm 63:2,3–4,5–6,8–9
John 20:1–2,11–18

There is no god besides you who have the care of all.
—WISDOM 12:13

This statement from today's reading doesn't rule out other
gods, other little household spirits that attempt to fend off
evil. It doesn't even rule out great gods that might preside
over Greece or Norway or India. It states very simply the
difference: there is only one god who has the care of all. I
recently met a nun, a new convert from Judaism, who in one
breath would talk about her love for Jesus and in the next
would say how she wants to learn about Islam and work with
refugees, not converting, she said, but serving and loving
them. It made me feel that we do indeed worship a god who
has the care of all.

Wisdom 12:13,16–19
Psalm 86:5–6,9–10,15–16 (5a)
Romans 8:26–27
Matthew 13:24–43 or 13:24–30

Lift up your staff and, with hand outstretched over the sea, split the sea in two.
—EXODUS 14:16

Our twenty-first-century world is rinsed of magic and miracle. That's one reason I love being part of an ancient and immense Church. In almost every reading we hear of wondrous deeds. Today it's Moses, standing like a great sorcerer on the edge of the sea, his hair and cape blown wild, his staff held high. Today we also celebrate St. Sharbel Makhluf, a Lebanese monk who spent twenty-three years as a hermit. Each night in front of the altar, he knelt ecstatic on a dish of canes, and when he died light shot out from his tomb. Some may dismiss all of this as fantasy or insanity, forgetting that ancient and immense force, great enough to split the seas and sustain our joy in solitude and death.

Exodus 14:5–18
Exodus 15:1bc–2,3–4,5–6
Matthew 12:38–42

"Can you drink the chalice that I am going to drink?"
They said to him, "We can."
—MATTHEW 20:22

We know very little of St. James. He was the first to follow
Jesus and the first to die, and once, scarcely knowing what he
meant, he chimed in with his brother and said, "We can."
Now, pilgrims trudge five hundred miles down St. James's
Way and say to themselves, "We can, we can," and try to
believe it. And when they finally reach Compostela, Spain, a
censor swings on silver ropes from the church ceiling, "the
whole length of the church," writes poet Anne Carson, "in
great fuming swerves that carry our prayer up to God and
drown the stench of new hearts as they burn below." Thank
God our church takes pity on our burning hearts and allows
these grand displays, for they help us say "We can" and
mean it.

2 Corinthians 4:7–15
Psalm 126:1bc–2ab,2cd–3,4–5,6
Matthew 20:20–28

• SS. JOACHIM AND ANNE, PARENTS OF THE BLESSED VIRGIN MARY •

This is the bread which the Lord has given you to eat.
—EXODUS 16:15

This story from Exodus 16 is so beautiful I want to quote it at
length: "In the morning a dew lay all about the camp, and
when the dew evaporated, there on the surface of the desert
were fine flakes like hoarfrost on the ground. On seeing it
the children of Israel asked one another, 'What is this?' . . .
But Moses told them, 'This is the bread which the Lord has
given you to eat.'" In our Mass we relive this moment. "Send
down your spirit like the dewfall," the priest prays. And later
he holds up a flake of bread, as delicate as hoarfrost, and
says, "Behold the Lamb of God." We kneel in our pews, in
our doubt, and wonder, "What is this?" And then we listen
over and over as the minister answers, "The body of Christ."

Exodus 16:1–5,9–15
Psalm 78:18–19,23–24,25–26,27–28
Matthew 13:1–9

JULY 27

Moses led the people out of the camp to meet God.
—EXODUS 19:17

Can you imagine going on a trip like the one Exodus describes today? "It's time to meet your maker," someone says, and you know they plan to kill you. That must have been how it felt to crouch at the foot of Mt. Sinai, like you were about to die, flame and smoke all around you, stinging your eyes, and a trumpet suddenly blasting in the midst of thunder, crushing your nerves. They must have wondered, *Is it the gates of Sheol or heaven?* It was nothing like those pastel paintings of angels blowing sweetly on long-necked horns. No wonder Jesus tells us today that we must be converted and healed before we can see the truth with our eyes and hear with our ears. It's the only way to bear what will no doubt feel like dying.

Exodus 19:1–2,9–11,16–20b
Daniel 3:52,53,54,55,56
Matthew 13:10–17

Hear the parable of the sower.
—MATTHEW 13:18

I was taken aback when I read in the parable today that a seed sown on rocky ground is the one who receives the Word with joy. Isn't receiving the Word with joy always a good thing? But Jesus says, "He has no root and lasts only for a time." I remember a moment from my childhood, the face of a girl on our camp bus as we sang, "Hey, Look Me Over." Closing her eyes, engrossed, she'd sing almost rapturously, "I'll be up on a rosebud, high on a vine." Oddly jealous, I'd try to copy her rapture but could only feel my own forced smile.

I know it's a slight example, but it seems reminiscent of all my jealousy, of coveting someone else's joy without making it my own. "Only the seed received with understanding falls on rich soil," Jesus says. But understanding is slow, internal, and can't be copied.

Exodus 20:1–17
Psalm 19:8,9,10,11
Matthew 13:18–23

*She said to him, "Yes, Lord. I have come to believe that you
are the Christ."*
—JOHN 11:27

I've always related to Martha, who seems to me like the older
sister. As John Wayne might have put it, "She reminds me of
me." Once when my family was arriving home after a long
trip away, my little sister ran up to our old car, "Oh, white
car!" she cried, "I could kiss you!" "Don't," I scolded, "you'll
get germs." It's the burden of the older child to accept
responsibility earlier than she might if she weren't next in
line. But with responsibility often comes an overly serious,
overly judging personality. I have no doubt that if Jesus came
to my home, I'd be rushing about cleaning and cooking. So I
look to Martha, who eventually declared, "I have come to
believe," to help me find my way.

Exodus 24:3–8
Psalm 50:1b–2,5–6,14–15
John 11:19–27 or Luke 10:38–42

God said, "Ask something of me and I will give it to you."
—1 KINGS 3:5

It sounds as if Solomon could ask for anything at all and God would grant his wish, as if God were nothing more than a genie. But then Solomon asks for an understanding heart, and God says, "Because you have asked for this—not for a long life, nor for riches, nor for the life of your enemies, . . . I do as you requested." The televangelist Joel Osteen tells an anecdote that has always infuriated me. He says his child got an ice cream cone but immediately lost a scoop. The shop promptly gave his weeping daughter another scoop for free. He uses this as a case in point for how God answers prayer. But God does not open every door. He doesn't give us all we ask. He only opens the doors and gives the gifts we truly need.

1 Kings 3:5,7–12
Psalm 119:57,72,76–77,127–128,129–130 (97a)
Romans 8:28–30
Matthew 13:44–52 or 13:44–46

Monday

JULY 31

It becomes a large bush and the "birds of the sky come and dwell in its branches."
—MATTHEW 13:32

Ignatius of Loyola was a Spanish knight who converted to Catholicism after being wounded in battle. He went on to found the Jesuits and write the *Spiritual Exercises*, one of the most influential books ever written about the quest for God.

A bishop once called Loyola's words the grains of the mustard seed mentioned in the Gospels. They might be "trifles in appearance," he said, "but of the greatest value in their effects." Here is just a scattering of those seeds: "Go forth and set the world on fire. Act as if everything depended on you, trust as if everything depended on God. He who goes about to reform the world must begin with himself, or he loses his labor. Laugh and grow strong."

Exodus 32:15–24,30–34
Psalm 106:19–20,21–22,23
Matthew 13:31–35

Tuesday

AUGUST 1

• ST. ALPHONSUS LIGUORI, BISHOP AND DOCTOR OF THE CHURCH •

The LORD used to speak to Moses face to face.
—EXODUS 33:11

"On the whole, I do not find Christians . . . sufficiently sensible of conditions," wrote Annie Dillard in *Teaching a Stone to Talk*. "Does anyone have the foggiest idea what sort of power we so blithely invoke?" She suggests that ushers should pass out life preservers and lash us to our pews, and she likens the experience of Mass to a precarious encampment on a polar ice floe. It reminds me of what we witness today, the Israelites camped in tents around Mt. Sinai, their days revolving around the coming and going of Moses and the coming and going of God. Moses processes out to his tent, and the people rise. God comes down in his cloud, and the people worship. It's not unlike Mass: the procession, the rising and kneeling, God coming down. Shall we lash ourselves to our pews?

Exodus 33:7–11; 34:5b–9,28
Psalm 103:6–7,8–9,10–11,12–13
Matthew 13:36–43

AUGUST 2

The Kingdom of heaven is like a treasure buried in a field.
—MATTHEW 13:44

An unearthed treasure is often called a treasure trove, but in ancient Roman law, such a discovery was termed a *thesauros*, or "storehouse." The word *thesaurus* eventually came to mean a storehouse of words, like a dictionary or an encyclopedia. So the Roman word makes for a beautiful translation: "The kingdom of heaven is like a *thesaurus*," and we picture a book of words, the Word of God, buried in a field. I love the image of the person who finds this treasure, so overwhelmed he can't quite figure out what to do. He digs it up and buries it again and rushes about trying to buy the whole lot. But even more, I love the image of the Word of God, the Logos, sown just beneath the surface, waiting to be found.

Exodus 34:29–35
Psalm 99:5,6,7,9
Matthew 13:44–46

AUGUST 3

Then the cloud covered the meeting tent, and the glory of the LORD filled the Dwelling.
—EXODUS 40:34

Moses has just made the ark, the tabernacle, to hold the commandments. It has poles along each side so that men can carry it on their shoulders as they journey and spread a tent over it when they stop. Often the cloud of God comes and settles down upon it, and if the cloud doesn't lift, they don't go forward. Did the ark grow too heavy with the presence of God? Or could they not rouse themselves from worship to walk? Or did they fear jostling God out of his dwelling? Imagine bearing that holiness up, how carefully you'd walk, how you'd watch the sky for clouds. Shouldn't we walk that way too, as we return from the altar, the weight of God on our tongues?

Exodus 40:16–21,34–38
Psalm 84:3,4,5–6a and 8a,11
Matthew 13:47–53

Friday

AUGUST 4

Blow the trumpet at the new moon,
at the full moon, on our solemn feast.
—PSALM 81:3

I recently "discovered" the Chicago artist Sallie Wolf. She's more of a naturalist, actually, keeping journals full of notes and watercolor sketches. For twenty years she's observed the moon, tracking its rising and setting and location in the sky. "I was determined to see what I could teach myself strictly by looking," she wrote on her blog, and began to record how the moon moved from a northerly winter position to a southerly summer position. Eventually she graphed these north-south shifts and noticed that they looked like Gregorian chant music. With the help of a composer friend she put the shifts of the moon, five years' worth, into a beautiful chant. Today's psalm says, "There shall be no strange god among you." The psalm is calling us to look around, blow a trumpet at the moon. But we're too busy to look much, as Sallie does, so the world and God remain strange.

Leviticus 23:1,4–11,15–16,27,34b–37
Psalm 81:3–4,5–6,10–11ab
Matthew 13:54–58

The earth has yielded its fruits;
God, our God, has blessed us.
—PSALM 67:7

There was an early ecclesiastical debate. Should Mary be called *Christokos*, or Christ bearer, or more grandly, *Theotokos*, Mother of God? Archbishop Nestorius believed divine nature could never mingle completely with human nature, so he tried to limit Mary to just the woman who bore Christ. But in the year 431, the Council of Ephesus declared this view heresy, akin to denying the Incarnation. They restored the title of *Theotokos* and rededicated the Basilica of St. Mary Major to the Mother of God. And legend has it that at some point snow fell in summer on the basilica. Snow in winter is harsh and expected, but in summer it comes gently, a strange mingling of elements. So for years people tossed white rose petals from the basilica dome to honor Mary, in whose body God mingled with man.

Leviticus 25:1,8–17
Psalm 67:2–3,5,7–8
Matthew 14:1–12

Sunday

AUGUST 6

• THE TRANSFIGURATION OF THE LORD •

"Lord, it is good that we are here. If you wish, I will make three tents here, one for you, one for Moses, and one for Elijah"
—MATTHEW 17:4

This same bumbling line of Peter's occurs in all three accounts of the Transfiguration. I'm thankful none of those accounts tried to make Peter look more put together. For standing before a vision as dazzling as the sun, he doesn't make some profound proclamation but tries to think of something nice to say. "It is good that we are here," he offers, and you have to picture Moses, Elijah, and Jesus shining there, mind-blowingly glorious. "Um, can we make you guys some tents?" The contrast makes me laugh out loud. And yet what better thing is there to say? We are set down here in this life, allowed to see the sun rise and to love one another. It is good that we are here.

Daniel 7:9–10,13–14
Psalm 97:1–2,5–6,9
2 Peter 1:16–19
Matthew 17:1–9

AUGUST 7

Would that we had meat for food!
—NUMBERS 11:4

Just recently the children of Israel were happy. They were free and manna rained from the sky. But now they're pining for their days of slavery. "We remember the fish we used to eat without cost in Egypt," they say, "the cucumbers, the melons, the leeks, the onions, and the garlic." Manna had to be ground up only to make oily cakes. Economist Robert H. Frank has said that "even when the changes [in people's lives] are huge—positive or negative—most people adapt much more quickly and completely than they expected." And then happiness migrates back to previous levels. Yet it turns out it wasn't all the Israelites who complained, only the riffraff, Scripture calls them. And the others? They must have found ways to get off the hedonic treadmill, to remember where they were from and where they were going.

Numbers 11:4b–15
Psalm 81:12–13,14–15,16–17
Matthew 14:13–21

Tuesday

AUGUST 8

• ST. DOMINIC, PRIEST •

O you of little faith, why did you doubt?
—MATTHEW 14:31

Surrounding the recent miracles in Matthew—walking on water and multiplying the loaves and fishes—Jesus has been trying to go off alone. He has just learned of the death of John the Baptist and is grieving. "He withdrew in a boat to a deserted place by himself," Matthew told us yesterday, and today, "He went up on the mountain by himself to pray." I keep thinking that his grief must have seeped somehow into his miracles. Did the bread and fish taste of sadness? Was the water Jesus called Peter across a sea of tears? Maybe Peter felt that grief, the grief of mortality, and began to sink, but Jesus stretched out his hand and caught him. It was never grief alone but grief continually mixed with and buoyed up by hope.

Numbers 12:1–13
Psalm 51:3–4,5–6ab,6cd–7,12–13
Matthew 14:22–36 or 15:1–2,10–14

AUGUST 9

• ST. TERESA BENEDICTA OF THE CROSS, VIRGIN AND MARTYR •

*They gave way to craving in the desert
and tempted God in the wilderness.*
—PSALM 106:14

Lately, there have been many books about food and God. "We were made to crave," writes author Lysa TerKeurst. The problem is not craving itself—that's inevitable—but what we crave. Another author, Geneen Roth, puts it like this: "People turn to food when they are not hungry because they are hungry for something they can't name: a connection to what is beyond the concerns of daily life. Something deathless, something sacred." All of this revolves around what Jesus said when he was tempted in the desert: "One does not live by bread alone but by every word that comes forth from the mouth of God." When we come to realize the true source of our hunger, we can point our craving in the right direction.

Numbers 13:1–2,25–14:1,26a–29a,34–35
Psalm 106:6–7ab,13–14,21–22,23
Matthew 15:21–28

⇉256⇇

Thursday
AUGUST 10

• ST. LAWRENCE, DEACON AND MARTYR •

Lavishly he gives to the poor;
his generosity shall endure forever.
—PSALM 112:9

St. Lawrence was supposedly the archdeacon of Rome, in
charge of the treasury, but when the pope was executed, the
new prefect demanded that Lawrence turn over the church's
riches. Lawrence asked for three days to accomplish this and
immediately went out and collected a great number of
crippled, blind, and leprous individuals. When the prefect
came, Lawrence said without irony, "These are the treasures
of the church." For this he was put to death, slow-cooked
over a fire. One commentator said that though these stories
of St. Lawrence might be legend, "the greatest fact of his life
is certain: He died for Christ." And for this reason some
Catholics still look up at the Perseid meteor shower that
comes this time of year and think of him. The shooting stars
become not just bits of stellar dust burning up but the fire
that killed him and his falling tears.

2 Corinthians 9:6–10
Psalm 112:1–2,5–6,7–8,9
John 12:24–26

AUGUST 11

• ST. CLARE, VIRGIN •

What can one give in exchange for his life?
—MATTHEW 16:26

Today I'm thinking of my daughter Clare. When you lose
someone before she's born, it feels like an almost total loss, so
I've loved Pope Benedict's idea that we are not closed
monads, cut off from others. "We are not just ourselves," he
writes, "we are ourselves only as being in others." Then I
came across this today in *Scientific American*: "Cells may
migrate through the placenta between the mother and the
fetus, taking up residence in many organs of the body." The
article goes on: "We are accustomed to thinking of ourselves
as singular autonomous individuals, and these foreign cells
seem to suggest that most people carry remnants of other
individuals." This all seems relevant to St. Clare's prayer,
which I keep on my desk: "I, Clare, a servant of Christ, bless
you during my life and after my death, as I am able."

Deuteronomy 4:32–40
Psalm 77:12–13,14–15,16 and 21
Matthew 16:24–28

Take care not to forget the LORD.
—DEUTERONOMY 6:12

In the 1965 film *Shenandoah*, Jimmy Stewart gives this amusing dinner prayer: "Lord, we cleared this land. We plowed it, sowed it, and harvested it. We worked dog-bone hard for every crumb and morsel, but we thank you Lord just the same for the food we're about to eat, amen." How easy it is to slip into this mood, that life is hard and we've done it ourselves. God in his distant, invisible heaven can seem superfluous, until we remember that we arrived in a world, breathe air, and receive love we did not make. "Love the LORD, your God," Moses cries and tells us to drill these words into our children, speak of them at home and abroad, bind them at our wrists as a sign, and write them on our doorposts and fences. "Take care," Moses urges us, "not to forget."

Deuteronomy 6:4–13
Psalm 18:2–3a,3bc–4,47 and 51
Matthew 17:14–20

Sunday

AUGUST 13

• NINETEENTH SUNDAY IN ORDINARY TIME •

*After the fire there was a tiny whispering sound. When he heard this,
Elijah hid his face in his cloak.*
—1 KINGS 19:12–13

This whole sequence begins with a command: "Go outside
and stand on the mountain," the voice says. "The LORD will
be passing by." So Elijah goes and stands on the mountain,
exposed to the elements. Great winds and earthquakes and
fires come and still he stands there, waiting. Finally there's a
tiny whispering sound and only then does Elijah take cover.
This passage says two things about prayer. We must wait for
God in silence or we'll miss him as he passes by. And also,
even if we don't hide our faces, we should realize that it's the
Lord of the universe, more fearsome than wind and fault lines
and fire, whom we kneel before.

1 Kings 19:9a,11–13a
Psalm 85:9,10,11–12,13–14 (8)
Romans 9:1–5
Matthew 14:22–33

What does the LORD, your God, ask of you . . . ?
—DEUTERONOMY 10:12

When Maximilian Kolbe was a child, Mary came to him in a dream and held out a white crown of purity and a red crown of martyrdom. "Which are you willing to accept?" she asked. He answered, "Both." Years later, after running a hospital, sheltering Jews during the Holocaust, and issuing anti-Nazi publications, Kolbe was taken as Prisoner No. 16670 to Auschwitz. At some point, ten prisoners were selected to be starved in an underground bunker. One man cried out, "My wife! My children!" and Kolbe asked to go in his place. Kolbe was the last to remain alive, and every time the guard checked on him, he was kneeling in his cell. He was finally killed by an injection of carbolic acid. "The most deadly poison of our time is indifference," Kolbe once said. "A single act of love makes the soul return to life."

Deuteronomy 10:12–22
Psalm 147:12–13,14–15,19–20
Matthew 17:22–27

Tuesday

AUGUST 15

• THE ASSUMPTION OF THE BLESSED VIRGIN MARY •

Blessed are you among women, and blessed is the fruit of your womb.
—LUKE 1:42

Many people think that the Assumption of Mary is meant to suggest that, instead of dying, Mary just floated up into the clouds. But even the statement of the dogma—"having completed the course of her earthly life"—leaves open the possibility that Mary died a natural, human death. In fact, the Eastern Church today celebrates the Dormition, or falling asleep, of Mary. The traditional icon depicts Mary laid out on a bier with Jesus standing over her and holding what looks like a small, swaddled infant—but really it is Mary's soul. It's such a beautiful reversal of the image of Madonna and Child, and it brings home the power of Mary for us. In Mary we see ourselves, how Christ might live inside of us and how we, mortal beings that we are, might live in Christ.

VIGIL:
1 Chronicles 15:3–4,15–16; 16:1–2
Psalm 132:6–7,9–10,13–14
1 Corinthians 15:54b–57
Luke 11:27–28

DAY:
Revelation 11:19a; 12:1–6a,10ab
Psalm 45:10,11,12,16
1 Corinthians 15:20–27
Luke 1:39–56

Where two or three are gathered together in my name, there am I in the midst of them.
—MATTHEW 18:20

So often I've noticed a new habit of speech in my children only to realize later it's my habit. My six-year-old recently started making this little head-nodding affirmation, "Mmmm," and I wondered where she'd picked it up, but soon I caught myself making this same sound. My friend described something similar, looking in the mirror once and seeing her mother's expression, the same set of jaw, looking back. My own mother once watched an old home movie and was shocked to recognize her own gestures in those of her long-gone mother. We cannot separate ourselves from those around us. We share our habits and voices and loves. So even when God comes to us in our apparent solitude, he still stands in our midst, in the midst of those we have gathered within us.

Deuteronomy 34:1–12
Psalm 66:1–3a,5 and 8,16–17
Matthew 18:15–20

AUGUST 17

This is how you will know that there is a living God in your midst.
—JOSHUA 3:10

The Ark of the Covenant of the Lord of the whole earth will precede the people of God into the Jordan. The people will stand at the flooded banks and wonder how they could ever cross, but the ark will continue on. And unbelievably, the water will stand back in a solid mass and leave the riverbed bare and appalled in the sun, and it will let the people pass. This story from Joshua is beautiful all by itself. But now read it again and think: we are the people of God and Christ is the ark. It's only by following that ark into uncertain waters that we will know there is a living God in our midst.

Joshua 3:7–10a,11,13–17
Psalm 114:1–2,3–4,5–6
Matthew 18:21–19:1

AUGUST 18

Give thanks to the God of gods.
—PSALM 136:2

Using the Hebrew words for *God* and *gods*, this psalm would
have read: Give thanks to the *Elohim* of *elohim*. *Elohim* is the
most common word used for God in the Old Testament, the
plural form of *El*, which means "The Strong One." Scholars
say it is the majestic plural, or the royal *we*, but they also note
that it hints at the Trinity. I like the idea implicit in this line
from the psalm, that the one God does not eradicate other
gods, only supersedes them. For as soon as we stop believing
in the gods in the moon and stars and trees, it becomes easy
to believe in a world devoid of mystery, with no God at all.
So let us instead give thanks to Elohim, the three in one, who
is the source of all powers that be.

Joshua 24:1–13
Psalm 136:1–3,16–18,21–22 and 24
Matthew 19:3–12

Saturday

AUGUST 19

• ST. JOHN EUDES, PRIEST •

Children were brought to Jesus that he might lay his hands on them and pray.
—MATTHEW 19:13

There is something about the head of a newborn and even a little child that calls out for everyone to lay their hand upon it. Our hands are irresistibly beckoned by that newness and warmth. And even now when we are so careful to respect one another's personal space, apologizing when our coat sleeve might brush up against another's, we still reach across that boundary to touch a child's head. In this we see something fundamental. Beneath all our cultural caution, we yearn to touch one another, to bless and be blessed.

Joshua 24:14–29
Psalm 16:1–2a and 5,7–8,11
Matthew 19:13–15

*My house shall be called
a house of prayer for all peoples.*
—ISAIAH 56:7

The Hasidic leader Rabbi Nachman of Bratslav, Ukraine,
once said, "If a dead person were allowed to return to this
world and pray, you can be sure that he would pray with all
his might." The next time you kneel in Mass, don't think only
of the people you are praying for and the people around you
praying their separate prayers. Think also of the communion
of saints that prays with us. For we can be sure that even if
we aren't praying with all our might, they are.

Isaiah 56:1,6–7
Psalm 67:2–3,5,6,8 (4)
Romans 11:13–15,29–32
Matthew 15:21–28

All these I have observed. What do I still lack?
—MATTHEW 19:20

What do I lack? It is the question at the center of all of our lives. No matter how rich we are, no matter how good, the question remains. Today Jesus gives the only answer that has ever sufficed: "Come, follow me." For, as Augustine puts it, our hearts are restless until they rest in God.

Judges 2:11–19
Psalm 106:34–35,36–37,39–40,43ab and 44
Matthew 19:16–22

Tuesday

AUGUST 22

• THE QUEENSHIP OF THE BLESSED VIRGIN MARY •

Truth shall spring out of the earth.
—PSALM 85:11

Recently a friend brought up her biggest stumbling block to
Catholicism. "Talk to me about Mary," she said. I wasn't sure
how to respond. Some religious groups seem to be trying to
scrub Christianity clean of superstition. Maybe for them
Mary is too much associated with crowns and statues and
beads and they'd prefer to let her fade away into the
background. It's as if they want to leave her back in the
grotto and let Christ walk out alone. But isn't this almost like
chasing him out of our world altogether? God allowed
himself to be born of a woman, to take on her features no
less. Did he have her eyes? What I should have said to my
friend is that if we call her queen, it's because we wish to
gaze upon her and imagine how Christ might shine from our
faces too.

Judges 6:11–24a
Psalm 85:9,11–12,13–14
Matthew 19:23–30

⇒269⇐

Come and take refuge in my shadow.
—JUDGES 9:15

Today's reading is the parable of the trees, as the olive and fig and bramble all stand in for people. I recently learned that we are connected to trees in surprising ways, sharing as much as 50 percent of our DNA and processing sugars in a similar way. A new company has started encoding the DNA of people into trees, creating what they call "transgenic tombstones." But parables and science aside, I think we have always identified with trees, which stand as ancient witnesses to our lives. In south-central Utah, there's a grove of quaking aspen, known as the Trembling Giant, that has lived for more than 80,000 years. Poet Wendell Berry refers to the "standing Sabbath of the woods," and it's beautiful to think of all the earth's trillions of trees, unmoving and sleepless, praying even before anyone was here.

Judges 9:6–15
Psalm 21:2–3,4–5,6–7
Matthew 20:1–16

Thursday

AUGUST 24

• ST. BARTHOLOMEW, APOSTLE •

How do you know me?
—JOHN 1:48

Today we celebrate one of the lesser-known apostles, St. Bartholomew, who some scholars think is also known by the name Nathanael in the gospels. Philip finds Nathanael and says, "Come and see." When they reach Jesus, Nathanael gets the feeling that Jesus already knows him. "How do you know me?" he asks. And Jesus says simply, "I saw you under the fig tree." Nathanael is stunned. The fig tree is back where he'd just been, quite a ways away. Jesus couldn't have been there. Nathanael tries to remember what he'd been doing under the fig tree. Maybe praying, with his eyes closed. And then he realizes that Jesus truly *saw* him, his whole self, the yearning of his heart, maybe his feelings of hopelessness, his love. "Rabbi, you are the Son of God," he exclaims. "Come and see" is the call to conversion. And what are we to see? That we are already truly and deeply seen.

Revelation 21:9b–14
Psalm 145:10–11,12–13,17–18
John 1:45–51

⇒ 271 ⇐

Love your neighbor as yourself.
—MATTHEW 22:39

Sometimes my six-year-old likes to type what she calls silly words on a keyboard. But yesterday I opened my computer to find this message: "I love you momy I dipend on you." I've been thinking about this and about what Jesus says today, that the whole law and the prophets depend on the commandments to love the Lord and love your neighbor as yourself. Everything depends on love, and we hold this love for one another. Even though I didn't grow up explicitly religious, my parents gave me such a profound love that I've believed in eternity all my life. I sat on my daughter's bed last night, stroking her forehead, feeling her little brow while she was "dipending" on me, and marveled that the enormous love that once made me feel like my parents were gods was now mine to give to someone else.

Ruth 1:1,3–6,14b–16,22
Psalm 146:5–6ab,6c–7,8–9a,9bc–10
Matthew 22:34–40

AUGUST 26

Naomi took the child, placed him on her lap, and became his nurse.
—RUTH 4:16

Ruth's declaration to Naomi, "Wherever you go, I will go," is such a beautiful line, such a creed of love, that it's hard to remember anything else about the story. At the start Ruth is newly widowed, cut off from her family, and Naomi has lost her sons. They come together in their grief. Ruth eventually marries into Naomi's family, so when her son Obed is born, he's related to both of them. The last significant line in the story is this: "Naomi took the child, placed him on her lap, and became his nurse." She is treating the child as if he were her own. And so the opening advance, "wherever you go, I will go," is now met with, "whomever you love, I will love." So though they're only friends, Ruth and Naomi become one through love.

Ruth 2:1–3,8–11; 4:13–17
Psalm 128:1b–2,3,4,5
Matthew 23:1–12

AUGUST 27

• TWENTY-FIRST SUNDAY IN ORDINARY TIME •

He asked his disciples, "Who do people say that the Son of Man is?"
—MATTHEW 16:13

Now, millennia after the birth of Christ, answers to this
question—Who do people say that the Son of Man
is?—abound. There are so many theories that now Jesus
could literally be anyone: God, a lunatic, a great teacher, a
charlatan, a prophet, an alien, a man. It would be easy to
leave this question to scholars and imagine it was never
meant for us. And yet his first question is followed closely by
a second: "But who do *you* say that I am?" No other person in
human history demands that we answer such a question. It
can be maddening. How are we expected to understand such
a long-ago, disputed person? Can't we just let this mystery
be? And yet, the question is out there. Anyone who has ever
heard this question returns to it again and again throughout
his life, even if only in the silence of his own thoughts.

Isaiah 22:19–23
Psalm 138:1–2,2–3,6,8 (8bc)
Romans 11:33–36
Matthew 16:13–20

*You do not enter yourselves, nor do you allow entrance to those
trying to enter.*
—MATTHEW 23:13

"Men go abroad to admire the heights of mountains . . . and
the circuits of the stars," wrote St. Augustine, "yet pass over
the mystery of themselves without a thought." Augustine was
one of the first people to use writing to look inside himself
for the truth that lies in all of us. It was this humble quest
that led him to say, "Late have I loved you, beauty so old and
so new . . . and see, you were within and I was in the external
world and sought you there. . . . You were with me, and I was
not with you." If we never enter ourselves, we'll never find
what's hidden there. But better for us to come late than never
to that Love, which has loved us from the start.

1 Thessalonians 1:1–5,8b–10
Psalm 149:1b–2,3–4,5–6a and 9b
Matthew 23:13–22

We were determined to share with you not only the Gospel of God, but our very selves as well.
—1 THESSALONIANS 2:8

There are countless paintings of St. John's beheading, countless heads dripping with blood. We have to wonder why this gruesome moment drew such attention. John the Baptist's life was a single cry, a "make straight the way of the Lord" to try to get us to see the truth. So did artists see in his death a similar scream? We look on, with all those spectators in the paintings, and see not only his death but also the fact of death laid out cold and inescapable on a platter. And maybe that is what these images are telling us. It's only by facing death that we can see the one coming toward us and say, as John did, "Behold, the Lamb of God who takes away the sin of the world."

1 Thessalonians 2:1–8
Psalm 71:1–2,3–4a,5–6ab,15ab and 17
Mark 6:17–29

AUGUST 30

Where can I go from your spirit?
—PSALM 139:7

The wisdom of Zen Buddhism is beautiful. Jon Kabat-Zinn, author of *Wherever You Go, There You Are*, writes, "There is just this moment. We are not trying to improve or get anywhere else." Words like these center us and bring our racing minds and bodies into stillness. But here's the problem I always run into. What will we find in that stillness? Here's Kabat-Zinn's answer: "At the deepest level, there is no giver, no gift, and no recipient . . . only the universe rearranging itself." It is this belief that disturbs me. I certainly don't want to dwell in a moment that involves nothing. No me. No anyone else. The psalm today gives a different answer. We can stop racing about because wherever we go, there God is, and even the night shines as the day.

1 Thessalonians 2:9–13
Psalm 139:7–8,9–10,11–12ab
Matthew 23:27–32

AUGUST 31

Jesus said to his disciples: "Stay awake!"
—MATTHEW 24:42

And Paul writes to the Thessalonians, "Night and day we pray beyond measure." How is it possible that even at night, every night, we should stay on the alert? Contemplative nuns and monks solve this problem by consecrating their sleep to God. At Compline they sing the "Nunc Dimittis," as gentle as any lullaby: "Protect us, Lord, as we stay awake; watch over us as we sleep, that awake, we may keep watch with Christ, and asleep, rest in his peace." When we are little, someone sits by our beds, strokes our heads, and sings. But as adults, we have to find our own way into sleep. Tonight, if you pray the "Nunc Dimittis," know that you are not alone. All around the world, at Compline everywhere, the Church is singing with you, as surely as a mother by your bed.

1 Thessalonians 3:7–13
Psalm 90:3–5a,12–13,14 and 17
Matthew 24:42–51

Give us some of your oil, for our lamps are going out.
—MATTHEW 25:8

In this parable from Matthew, ten virgins are waiting for the *parousia*, the presence or arrival, of the bridegroom. Many interpret this as the second coming of Christ, but I think it offers a more pressing message. In some sense we are perpetually encountering *parousia*, for God is always near at hand. But since we come in and out of awareness of God, his presence can sometimes feel like a sudden arrival, even though really it's we who have arrived. In this way, the oil becomes that which keeps us perpetually arriving, that which fuels the wick of our spirit. Even though we hold our faith communally, faith can never completely transcend individual belief. We become ourselves only through and with others, but we are still ourselves, unique in all the world, and each of us carries her own lamp.

1 Thessalonians 4:1–8
Psalm 97:1 and 2b,5–6,10,11–12
Matthew 25:1–13

Aspire to live a tranquil life.
—1 THESSALONIANS 4:11

The word *aspire* seems to indicate motion, an urgent, clambering desire, and yet *aspire* literally means "to breathe" or "to breathe in desire for." How different it sounds now—*breathe in desire for a tranquil life*—so internal and heartfelt. It still might seem like a bit of vague New Age wisdom, breathing in peace and breathing out stress, but Paul goes on. "Mind your own affairs," he adds, "and work with your own hands." Now we have a fuller portrait of the good life, a life not caught up in external striving, in gossip, in fruitless labors, but rather in its own private demands. So breathe in desire for a tranquil life. Mind your own affairs. Work with your own hands.

1 Thessalonians 4:9–11
Psalm 98:1,7–8,9
Matthew 25:14–30

SEPTEMBER 3

You duped me, O LORD, and I let myself be duped.
—JEREMIAH 20:7

Once when I was visiting the Abbey of Gethsemani, one of the monks told us that another Trappist monastery had collectively decided to leave out the curses in the psalms and pray only the nice parts. He said how much less human that would make the psalms, how much less like our own prayers. Today let's give thanks for Jeremiah's glorious curses. If we allow ourselves his honesty, declaring, "I will speak in his name no more!" we'll see that God doesn't just disappear but becomes, as Jeremiah tells us, a fire burning in our heart, imprisoned in our bones, and in this way more real. And really that's what we were after in the first place, to know that God is really here, in our hearts, in our bones, no matter what.

Jeremiah 20:7–9
Psalm 63:2,3–4,5–6,8–9 (2b)
Romans 12:1–2
Matthew 16:21–27

SEPTEMBER 4

• LABOR DAY •

We do not want you to be unaware, brothers and sisters, about those who have fallen asleep, so that you may not grieve like the rest, who have no hope.

—1 THESSALONIANS 4:13

I live near Rosehill, the largest cemetery in Chicago—more than three hundred acres of land reserved for burying the dead. I often walk there and read the epitaphs. The saddest one is for Lulu Fellows, who died at age sixteen. "Many hopes lie buried here," it says. Roman epitaphs often took a similarly despairing tone. "How quickly we fall back from nothing to nothing," reads a Roman one. Our faith, our hope, comes down to one thing, eternal life, so we begin our life in the Church at baptism with this dialogue: "What do you ask of the Church?" says the priest. "Faith," say the parents. "And what does faith give you?" he asks. "Eternal life," they say, cradling the head of their child in hope.

1 Thessalonians 4:13–18
Psalm 96:1 and 3,4–5,11–12,13
Luke 4:16–30

SEPTEMBER 5

What is there about his word?
—LUKE 4:36

We are living in a secular age, two thousand seventeen years after the birth of Christ. The words of Christianity—our terms for God and Jesus and heaven and salvation—have been used and overused, and now to many they sound old-fashioned and clownish. And to even us, who profess belief in the Word, this language can come off as worn out or impossible. We must try instead to listen, like the people in today's Gospel, who were hearing this language for the first time. "What is there about his word?" they whispered to each other.

1 Thessalonians 5:1–6,9–11
Psalm 27:1,4,13–14
Luke 4:31–37

I, like a green olive tree,
in the house of God,
Trust in the mercy of God.
—PSALM 52:10

This passage reads like a haiku poem. Each line is five to seven syllables in length, there are two contrasting images, a green olive tree and the house of God, and it begins with the quick, startling association of "I" with a tree. The olive tree was the first sign of life after the Flood and the symbol of peace, so it stands at the center of salvation history. And we can think of salvation history as just another name for God's house. But this same tree, the poem says, also trusts in the mercy of God; it's both the sign of mercy and the recipient of mercy. So in the olive tree we see both Christ and ourselves. And isn't that how we'll manage to stand in God's house at all, within the green foliage of Christ's peace?

Colossians 1:1–8
Psalm 52:10,11
Luke 4:38–44

SEPTEMBER 7

"Depart from me, Lord, for I am a sinful man."
—LUKE 5:8

Simon Peter cannot look into the future. He cannot see how
much he will come to love this Lord. He cannot know that
he'll have to watch him die. And he cannot imagine that
future day when, heartsick and lost, he will take out his boat
again, just like he did today, pull up another great catch, and
then incredibly turn to see the Lord waiting for him on the
shore. He cannot see any of this, but he can feel it, so he falls
down at the knees of the Lord and begs, "Depart from me."
But Jesus says gently, "Do not be afraid." And Peter leaves
everything and follows him. We cannot know our future; we
can only follow the one who holds it.

Colossians 1:9–14
Psalm 98:2–3ab,3cd–4,5–6
Luke 5:1–11

She was found with child through the Holy Spirit.
—MATTHEW 1:18

I have this childhood memory that I remember as bathed in light. My mother is wearing one of her long, gauzy, white nightgowns, and I'm lying over her body in our soft rocking chair in front of our huge picture window. She's rocking me back and forth and whispering, "Big rocks, little rocks." Every single time I rock my own children, I remember that sensation of being held, enveloped in loveliness and love, so safely and sweetly rocked. In my arms I feel hers and am at once both child and mother. When Mary first held her new son, she must have felt that too, an almost physical sensation of her own mother's presence, and the sense of being there and here simultaneously. So in the nativity of Christ we glimpse, like a sketch beneath paint, the nativity of Mary.

Micah 5:1–4a or Romans 8:28–30
Psalm 13:6ab,6c
Matthew 1:1–16,18–23 or 1:18–23

SEPTEMBER 9

• ST. PETER CLAVER, PRIEST •

O God, hear my prayer;
hearken to the words of my mouth.
—PSALM 54:4

Hearken is a word we hardly ever use anymore. Even its definition in the dictionary sounds archaic: "to apply the ears to hear; to give ear." But hearken has a different nuance than just listening. It includes a preparatory act. Before we can properly listen we must prick up our ears, we must ready them, and then give them over to the task of listening. And really it's not God who must do this, but us. "Oh, that my people would hearken unto me," says Psalm 81, "and walk in my ways."

Colossians 1:21–23
Psalm 54:3–4,6 and 8
Luke 6:1–5

SEPTEMBER 10

• TWENTY-THIRD SUNDAY IN ORDINARY TIME •

For where two or three are gathered together in my name, there am I in the
midst of them.
—MATTHEW 18:20

What really brought me to the point of becoming Catholic
was a friend, who became my sponsor, and my husband, who
converted with me. Sometimes I worry that I converted
because of them. Similarly, when my mother became
Catholic, I worried she was converting out of love for me
rather than out of conviction. When I told my husband this,
he was horrified. "Love is an excellent reason to convert!" he
said, almost scolding. So whenever I fall back into those
worries, I remember his words and know he is right. The
gathering is what reveals the presence of Christ.

Ezekiel 33:7–9
Psalm 95:1–2,6–7,8–9 (8)
Romans 13:8–10
Matthew 18:15–20

SEPTEMBER 11

Only in God be at rest, my soul.
—PSALM 62:6

Recently I've been reading Frances Hodgson Burnett's *A Little Princess* to my children. The heroine, introspective Sara Crewe, starts out wealthy but is suddenly orphaned and reduced to being a penniless maid. "You see, now that trials have come, they have shown that I am not a nice child," she tells a friend. "I was afraid they would. Perhaps that is what they are for." But later she finds her strength. "It would be easy to be a princess if I were dressed in cloth of gold," she tells herself, "but it is a great deal more of a triumph to be one all the time when no one knows it." Her goodness becomes something internal. She prays in secret. She slips off to the attic to watch the sunrise alone. Her soul is in that place of rest that nothing else can touch.

Colossians 1:24–2:3
Psalm 62:6–7,9
Luke 6:6–11

SEPTEMBER 12

• THE MOST HOLY NAME OF MARY •

I will bless your name forever and ever.
—PSALM 145:2

The name of someone we love becomes more than a word. It seems to hold a person's being. When my son John was born, I listened over and over to Sinéad O'Connor's song "John, I Love You." The name John, she sings, is a whisper. And when my daughter Margaret was born, I bought pearl earrings, because her name means "pearl." Ever since Bethlehem, people have studied Mary's name. It's been associated with various Egyptian and Hebrew and Aramaic roots, each word yielding new meanings: bitter, beloved, cherished, mournful, drop of sea. Scholars argue over which etymology is correct, but the Church takes them all. And so we repeat, as if by saying her name we could touch her: Mary, Full of Grace, Mother of God, Lady of Sorrows, O Clement, O Loving, O Sweet, Star of the Sea.

Colossians 2:6–15
Psalm 145:1b–2,8–9,10–11
Luke 6:12–19

⇒ 290 ⇐

Think of what is above, not of what is on earth.
—COLOSSIANS 3:2

Paul begins this passage in his letter to the Colossians by
setting up the spirit-body problem. "If you were raised with
Christ, seek what is above," he says. I imagine he means that
I'm stuck in this low place with my wretched body and I must
send my spirit up to meet God in the air. I'm not always
happy with my body, but I like being able to walk and touch
things and hear. In Paul's next image, we are no longer
reaching for the air but for something closer at hand. "Take
off the old self," he says, "and put on the new." Now at least
my spirit is as close as a coat. But his final image erases any
distance: "Christ is all and in all." Now there's no movement
away, no separation, for that spirit I sought in the air and
tried to wrap about myself has suffused the world.

Colossians 3:1–11
Psalm 145:2–3,10–11,12–13ab
Luke 6:20–26

*So must the Son of Man be lifted up, so that everyone who believes in
him may have eternal life.*
—JOHN 3:14–15

I always wonder what someone who knows nothing about
Christianity would make of Christ on the cross. It would
surely stand out from all other portraits of divinity. Instead of
an image of peace or power or grandeur, this person would
see a man nailed to a tree. "Yes," she might say, "I see the
truth of our lives, our tragedy. But why stare at it? Why not
try to forget?" Then we'd tell her the second part. After this
man died, he rose, and became the light of the world. The
cross gives us the deepest truth of human mortality paired
with our greatest hope. And I imagine even if this were all
you knew, it might haunt or tempt or even compel you all
your days.

Numbers 21:4b–9
Psalm 78:1bc–2,34–35,36–37,38
Philippians 2:6–11
John 3:13–17

And you yourself a sword will pierce.
—LUKE 2:35

One of our church's artists-in-residence, Joseph Malham, once described the Pietà as a spiritual riff on Scripture, for the Gospels never tell how the body of Jesus was laid out across Mary's lap. "The image is shockingly asymmetrical," Malham says. Jesus is not the center of the image; instead the lines draw our eyes to Mary's. Since we know what's coming, we tend to forget her grief, not only for her child but for the angels and the kingdom and all that lost possibility. If for an instant God was forsaken by God on the cross and Jesus left to fear he was only Adam, Mary was left to fear that her son was in fact mortal and that she was only Eve, the mother of death. In her eyes we see this ultimate fear and sorrow, which then allows us to turn and see the Resurrection for what it is.

1 Timothy 1:1–2,12–14
Psalm 16:1b–2a and 5,7–8,11
John 19:25–27 or Luke 2:33–35

SEPTEMBER 16

• SS. CORNELIUS, POPE, AND CYPRIAN, BISHOP, MARTYRS •

Who is like the LORD, our God,
and looks upon the heavens and the earth below?
—PSALM 113:5–6

Imagine that we could see God. A great pair of eyes looking down on us like suns. Or a back rounded like a sky over the world. Or just a cartoonish man seated on a cloud. If we could see God we could study him, size him up, and get past him. And this is exactly what many people think they've already done. But whatever images they have rejected—sun, sky, or cartoon god—it is not, as Paul calls him, the invisible, only God. God lies beyond the universe, outside heaven and earth, and all our tools of language and science cannot meet him there. Yet we have this hope that reaches out beyond mortality, beyond what is seen, that the Great Beyond came into the world, as Paul says today, to save us.

1 Timothy 1:15–17
Psalm 113:1b–2,3–4,5a and 6–7
Luke 6:43–49

Remember your last days, set enmity aside;
remember death and decay, and cease from sin!
—SIRACH 28:6

"Could anyone nourish anger against another," asks Sirach, "and expect healing from the LORD?" I remember when I was little, I used to get angry with my sister and swear to myself with furious conviction that I would never speak to her again, ever, ever. I can almost see how the glass looked on the bedroom window I used to glare through. I'd get even angrier at myself as I remembered all the times I'd failed to make good on this vow. But always after just a few minutes I'd get lonely and go look for her. The love in a family makes hatred impossible, canceling it out again and again. In the same way, the kingdom of God, that greater family of everyone, does not allow hatred. By hating you banish not someone else but yourself.

Sirach 27:30–28:7
Psalm 103:1–2,3–4,9–10,11–12 (8)
Romans 14:7–9
Matthew 18:21–35

SEPTEMBER 18

It is my wish, then, that in every place the men should pray, lifting up holy hands.

—1 TIMOTHY 2:8

These days we tend to associate hands held up in worship with charismatic Christians, but the gesture is as old as prayer, predating Christianity. It's called the *orans*, which means simply "the one who is praying." Usually the elbows are held close to the body, while the forearms stretch out, open-palmed. There are many early catacomb frescoes of the *orans*, now beautifully flaked, with bright patches of stone showing through like light. One portrays Moses on the ark, receiving the dove. Like kneeling, the *orans* is a gesture that seems natural to prayer, conveying at once pleading, the offering of oneself, and an openness to what comes. But for us, it's also an imitation of the cross. So let your body assume this ancient form and lift up your holy hands.

1 Timothy 2:1–8
Psalm 28:2,7,8–9
Luke 7:1–10

SEPTEMBER 19

• ST. JANUARIUS, BISHOP AND MARTYR •

The dead man sat up and began to speak, and Jesus gave him to his mother.
—LUKE 7:15

This scene recalls a similar one from Kings. A little boy died and Elijah placed his hands and eyes and mouth upon him and then the boy sat up in bed and sneezed. "Take your son," Elijah said to the boy's mother. Today it is almost the same.

We know a bit more about the mother, that she was widowed, had only one son who had died, and was bitterly weeping. But after Jesus put his hand on her son's coffin, "the dead man sat up and began to speak," and just as Elijah had done, Jesus gave the man to his mother. Our hope is not that the risen will be merely swept off to eternity but that someday they'll be delivered back into our arms.

1 Timothy 3:1–13
Psalm 101:1b–2ab,2cd–3ab,5,6
Luke 7:11–17

SEPTEMBER 20

Beloved: I am writing you, although I hope to visit you soon.
—1 TIMOTHY 3:14

Many of us no longer write letters. But once, if you were away, you had to sit down and write a letter in your own hand. "A letter written in absorbed silence," says essayist Vivian Gornick, "is an act of faith." It requires faith, she says, because you must be alone with your thoughts in the conjured presence of another person. The other person is not there, and yet letters are so intimate that Johann Wolfgang von Goethe called them "the most beautiful, the most immediate breath of life." This makes writing letters sound a little like praying. For to pray, we must also be alone in the intimate but invisible company of someone else. Maybe we struggle to pray in part because we've lost that solitary habit of sharing our thoughts, even when a response might be a long time coming.

1 Timothy 3:14–16
Psalm 111:1–2,3–4,5–6
Luke 7:31–35

SEPTEMBER 21

• ST. MATTHEW, APOSTLE AND EVANGELIST •

The heavens declare the glory of God.
—PSALM 19:2

A few lines later in this psalm it says, "He has pitched in them a tent for the sun." This means, commentators say, that God has placed the sun like a tabernacle in the sky. But when I first read this line from the psalm, I imagined instead God pitching a tent inside of us. And I'm not sure my reading is so far off, because we say in Mass, "I am not worthy that you should enter under my roof," turning our bodies into dwellings. Today we celebrate Matthew, who was a tax collector, the quintessential biblical example of someone whose house was not worthy. So next time you say "I am not worthy" and walk up to the altar, imagine as you walk back the tent God has pitched inside of you and the sun that now shelters there.

Ephesians 4:1–7,11–13
Psalm 19:2–3,4–5
Matthew 9:9–13

We brought nothing into the world, just as we shall not be able to take anything out of it.
—1 TIMOTHY 6:7

Today is my birthday. I've always taken a nerdy pleasure in sharing a birthday with the hobbits Bilbo and Frodo Baggins, the ring bearers of J. R. R. Tolkien's saga *Lord of the Rings*. "I wish the ring had never come to me," Frodo says at one point, and Gandalf replies, "So do all who live to see such times. But that is not for them to decide. All we have to decide is what to do with the time that is given to us." In today's readings we also hear of Joanna and Susanna, followers of Jesus, whom we don't meet again until they bring myrrh for Jesus' tomb. They're simply known as the myrrh bearers. In some ways it's a relief to think it's not up to us what heavy thing might come, only what we'll do when it's ours to bear.

1 Timothy 6:2c–12
Psalm 49:6–7,8–10,17–18,19–20
Luke 8:1–3

SEPTEMBER 23

• ST. PIUS OF PIETRELCINA, PRIEST •

As they go along, they are choked by the anxieties and riches and
pleasures of life, and they fail to produce mature fruit.
—LUKE 8:14

This verse reminds me of comedian Louis C.K.'s rant against
cell phones. He hates our constant frenzy to text on our
phones in order to stave off what he calls the "forever
empty," our fear that it's all for nothing and we're alone. At
any minute that awareness can start to come on, for "life is
tremendously sad," he says, "just by being in it." Then he
recounts a time when he stopped and let the sadness hit him
like a truck. "I pulled over and just cried," he says. "It was
beautiful." He describes how "happiness came rushing in to
meet the sadness." We must clear the way for what lies
beneath all our pleasures and riches and anxieties and allows
true growth.

1 Timothy 6:13–16
Psalm 100:1b–2,3,4,5
Luke 8:4–15

SEPTEMBER 24

Seek the LORD while he may be found,
call him while he is near.
—ISAIAH 55:6

The cosmic calendar compresses the entire history of the universe into a single calendar year. The big bang occurs at midnight on January 1. Dinosaurs don't appear until June, birds and flowers not until December. And then in the last sixty seconds, all of human life unfolds: agriculture, cities, the birth of Christ, us. One single life is at most one-fourth of a second. Might it feel like that from God's view? Today let us pray with St. Thérèse of Lisieux: "My life is an instant, a fleeting hour. My life is a moment, which swiftly escapes me. O my God, you know that on earth I have only today to love you." And we might add, only this second.

Isaiah 55:6–9
Psalm 145:2–3,8–9,17–18 (18a)
Philippians 1:20c–24,27a
Matthew 20:1–16a

SEPTEMBER 25

*Those that sow in tears
shall reap rejoicing.*
—PSALM 126:5

I've always hated a vision of heaven that leaves out sadness and effort. So much of our love in this world is expressed in tears. And even though we fear our work is fruitless, we hold it dear. We don't want paradise to be some blank, bright place where we will walk stripped of all our sweat and tears. No, if that's heaven, then leave us here with our toil and sorrow. But where did we get this notion of such an empty, numb heaven? Today the psalm describes what it might be like to enter the promised land: like coming back from the harvest, the memory of tears still fresh in our eyes, our arms still aching from work but full, and our mouths filled with laughter.

Ezra 1:1–6
Psalm 126:1b–2ab,2cd–3,4–5,6
Luke 8:16–18

Tuesday

SEPTEMBER 26

• SS. COSMAS AND DAMIAN, MARTYRS •

Your mother and brothers are standing outside and they wish to see you.
—LUKE 8:20

I imagine Jesus peering through the crowd, trying to catch a glimpse of Mary. How easy it would have been to walk out and just be her son again and let the crowds disperse. I imagine her then coming in and standing at the edge of all those people, as her statue often stands off to the side of our altars. He might have looked at her a minute, and everyone else's gaze would have turned too, and then he would say, "My mother and my brothers are those who hear the word of God and act on it." Mary is often called the type or model of the Church, for more than anyone she heard and acted on the word of God. By following her example, as Jesus suggests, we together become his mother, his brothers, his Church.

Ezra 6:7–8,12b,14–20
Psalm 122:1–2,3–4ab,4cd–5
Luke 8:19–21

SEPTEMBER 27

*He has given us new life to raise again the house of our God and restore
its ruins, and has granted us a fence.*
—EZRA 9:9

In this passage Ezra is talking about building the second
temple in Jerusalem, but to us this passage sounds like
resurrection. And I love the image of God granting us a
fence. St. Vincent de Paul thinks of this fence as prayer,
which he calls "an impregnable rampart . . . a mystical
arsenal, a Tower of David, which will furnish [us] with all
sorts of arms." But we must never think of this fence as
something that shields us from the world and behind which
we can hide. "Go to the poor," St. Vincent says, urging us
always to venture out. "And you will find God."

Ezra 9:5–9
Tobit 13:2,3–4a,4befghn,7–8
Luke 9:1–6

Who then is this about whom I hear such things?
—LUKE 9:9

Various rumors made it to Herod. "John has been raised from the dead!" some said. "Elijah has appeared!" said others. It would have been easy to pass off such absurd, grand claims as nothing more than superstition and the wishful thinking of the masses. Today, claims about Jesus can sound just as absurd, even sometimes to those of us who believe. But even when these claims are apparently dismissed, the question lingers on: "Who then is this about whom I hear such things?" Jesus stands alone in history, posing a question no one has ever been able to ignore.

Haggai 1:1–8
Psalm 149:1b–2,3–4,5–6a and 9b
Luke 9:7–9

SEPTEMBER 29

• SS. MICHAEL, GABRIEL, AND RAPHAEL, ARCHANGELS •

*War broke out in heaven; Michael and his angels battled against
the dragon.*
—REVELATION 12:7

It is Michaelmas, the feast of the archangels. Last year on this
day a group of mothers in my parish dyed silk capes yellow,
like the capes of angels, read the story of St. George and the
dragon, flew a dragon kite, and made a bonfire on the beach.

Today my husband and I took our children back to that
beach, and from the top of a sand hill we watched them run
over the dunes of Lake Michigan, sun bright on everything
and their capes fluttering. High up a dragon kite rode the
wind. Eventually in my children's lives, when doubt calls
glory into question, I hope they'll remember this experience
of gold on the water, on the wind, and streaming out behind
them, and think of how love once sat like a king and queen
on the highest dune, keeping watch.

Daniel 7:9–10,13–14 or Revelation 12:7–12a
Psalm 138:1–2ab,2cde–3,4–5
John 1:47–51

SEPTEMBER 30

*I, Zechariah, raised my eyes and looked: there was a man with a
measuring line in his hand.*
—ZECHARIAH 2:5

I love the combination here of the mundane and fantastic. I
just raised my eyes, the prophet said, and might have added,
"as if glancing up from a book." There stood a man holding a
measuring cord. He must have looked like a tailor or
surveyor, and we might imagine today some practical chap
with eyeglasses and a tool. But pretty soon he's joined by
others, and one declares, "I will be for her an encircling fire
for the city, and the glory in her midst." It makes it more
beautiful that these words come not from shining creatures
but from what look like regular men, as if angels could be
anywhere, stirring forth, as Zechariah says today, from God's
holy dwelling.

Zechariah 2:5–9,14–15a
Jeremiah 31:10,11–12ab,13
Luke 9:43b–45

Sunday

OCTOBER 1

• TWENTY-SIXTH SUNDAY IN ORDINARY TIME •

*If there is any encouragement in Christ, any solace in love, any
participation in the Spirit, any compassion and mercy . . .*
—PHILIPPIANS 2:1

Evil and good are not equal weights. We would never say, "If
there is any shred of evil, any glimpse of death, then all hope
is lost." And yet that's exactly what we say about goodness.
Think of the tree that becomes a symbol of life in the story
A Tree Grows in Brooklyn: "No matter where its seed fell, it
made a tree which struggled to reach the sky," wrote Betty
Smith. "It grew in boarded-up lots and out of neglected
rubbish heaps, and it was the only tree that grew out of
cement. It grew lushly." If we can see any bit of green, any
glimpse of sun, any encouragement, any love, then we still
have hope that a single life was enough to overcome
the darkness.

Ezekiel 18:25–28
Psalm 25:4–5,6–7,8–9 (6a)
Philippians 2:1–11 or 2:1–5
Matthew 21:28–32

⇒ 309 ⇐

Monday

OCTOBER 2

• THE HOLY GUARDIAN ANGELS •

I will rescue my people from the land of the rising sun, and from the land of the setting sun.
—ZECHARIAH 8:7

We live in that land, the land of birth and death. Today we're beautifully told that we'll be rescued from that place and that old men and old women, each with staff in hand, shall again sit in the streets, which will be filled with boys and girls playing. We're also told that the Lord of Hosts will bring this about. Hosts are angels, and today we celebrate the Holy Guardian Angels. Scripture suggests that we each have a guardian who will remain with us even in heaven. And I imagine we'll need our angels there, for it is said that all our time will come back to us, and incredibly we'll be both old and young at once, both those who sit with canes and those who play joyfully in the streets.

Zechariah 8:1–8
Psalm 102:16–18,19–21,29 and 22–23
Matthew 18:1–5,10

OCTOBER 3

*The inhabitants of one city will approach those of another, and say,
"Come! let us go to implore the favor of the LORD"; and "I too will go to
seek the LORD."*
—ZECHARIAH 8:20–21

Imagine opening your door to a person from, say, Uruguay
who says, "Come! Let us seek the Lord of Hosts." You'd wish
him well as you slammed the door. But then another might
come, from Malawi. "I too am going," she'd say. And then
others from Latvia, Togo, and Cambodia. Finally you might
open your door wide enough to see the street streaming with
pilgrims. But what I can't figure out is where they'd all be
going. Mt. Everest? To climb to the highest spot like in Dr.
Seuss and yell, "Yopp!" trying to be heard? Or is this instead
the afterlife, when the kingdoms of this world are gone and
everyone is headed to the feast?

Zechariah 8:20–23
Psalm 87:1b–3,4–5,6–7
Luke 9:51–56

Foxes have dens and birds of the sky have nests, but the Son of Man has nowhere to rest his head.
—LUKE 9:58

It is the way of abnegation that St. Francis so joyfully followed. If the Son of Man had nowhere to rest his head, then neither would St. Francis. He'd be lower than the animals. And maybe because of this humility, animals loved him. Legend has it that doves and crows and sparrows would gather and listen to him preach, spreading their wings and craning their necks. Rabbits would hop into his lap and refuse to leave, and fish would linger at the surface of the water. Even a wolf lowered his head like a lamb and placed his paw in the saint's palm as a pledge of peace. With our cars and houses and stores we've walled ourselves off from nature. Only in poverty and homelessness has that barrier ever been truly crossed.

Nehemiah 2:1–8
Psalm 137:1–2,3,4–5,6
Luke 9:57–62

OCTOBER 5

Hush, for today is holy, and you must not be saddened.
—NEHEMIAH 8:11

Life is loud, or at least mine is, with children in my house and the city of Chicago out my door. I used to listen to music when I drove, and now more often than not, I drive in silence. Well, not silence exactly, since I can always hear sirens and engines and trains. But in some sense these city sounds aren't the most damaging noise we face. The monk Thomas Merton talks about how we confound our lives with noise, stun our ears with meaningless words, shouting at death. We never discover, he says, that our hearts are rooted in a silence that is not death but life. Instead of seeking the absence of noise, we should seek this silence that always travels with us, beneath the noise. So hush, listen, for today is holy, and you must not be saddened.

Nehemiah 8:1–4a,5–6,7b–12
Psalm 19:8,9,10,11
Luke 10:1–12

Friday

OCTOBER 6

• ST. BRUNO, PRIEST • BLESSED MARIE-ROSE DUROCHER, VIRGIN •

O LORD, how long?
—PSALM 79:5

I once knew a woman with a large family and a busy job who longed to be a nun. "Just to be in all that silence and holiness," she said. She seemed to experience God in an almost visceral way. But then one day, God, who'd always been close, was suddenly gone. For two years she struggled with emptiness. "How long?" she must have prayed. She finally went to see a contemplative nun for spiritual direction. "Ask to know the Father," the nun told her. And then a little while later, when she was driving home from work, she looked up and saw nothing more than sun on a cloud, and God was back. Why did she have to struggle? Why did Mother Teresa also have to spend almost her entire life in such darkness? Only God knows what compassion, what sturdy longing, is learned when we believe ourselves to be left alone.

Baruch 1:15–22
Psalm 79:1b–2,3–5,8,9
Luke 10:13–16

As your hearts have been disposed to stray from God,
turn now ten times the more to seek him.
—BARUCH 4:28

Chains of beads have long been used for prayer. The word *bead* comes from the Middle English root *bede*, which means "prayer." In India there are similar beads called *japamala*. *Japa* means "chant," and *mala* is "rose garden." Our word *rosary* similarly means a plot of ground set aside for cultivating roses. Long ago, the desert hermits developed rhythmic motions to cultivate prayer, and they began praying the 150 psalms daily. The rosary, consisting of 150 beads, has been called the "poor man's breviary," a way for everyone to recall their prayers with repeated motions. But for many, it's simply a tool for stilling the mind. You hold a bead, say a Hail Mary or just the word *Jesus*, and turn ten times again, bead by bead, to seek him.

Baruch 4:5–12,27–29
Psalm 69:33–35,36–37
Luke 10:17–24

Sunday

OCTOBER 8

• TWENTY-SEVENTH SUNDAY IN ORDINARY TIME •

*In everything, by prayer and petitions, with thanksgiving, make your
requests known to God. Then the peace of God that surpasses all
understanding will guard your hearts and minds in Christ Jesus.*
—PHILIPPIANS 4:6

I've been thinking about the difference between acceptance
and peace. Acceptance means that you agree to what's on
offer. It may be good, or not so good, but you submit. Yet the
passage today does not indicate such a passive approach.
Instead, we're being urged to make our requests known in
everything—in other words, to petition God always about
what we haven't yet accepted. It's out of this fervent praying,
Paul says, that peace comes. I think meditation is a beautiful
idea, letting the mind quiet and God come in. But it's not the
only way to pray, or for that matter the only way to usher in
peace. We can also pound our fists and plead.

Isaiah 5:1–7
Psalm 80:9,12,13–14,15–16,19–20 (Isaiah 5:7a)
Philippians 4:6–9
Matthew 21:33–43

⇒ 316 ⇐

From the belly of the fish Jonah prayed to the LORD, his God.
—JONAH 2:1

I had remembered the fish in Jonah's story as a monster from
whose belly Jonah had to be rescued. But it wasn't like that.
Jonah was drowning. Breakers and billows passed over him,
seaweed wrapped around his head, and the deep enveloped
him. He began to die, which he described as his soul fainting
within him. But even then, Jonah called out, "How will I
again look upon your holy temple?" and the fish swallowed
him up (Jonah 2:5 NAB). The fish was his rescue, its belly a
dark little cell within the greater darkness of the sea, a place
of rest. We spend our lives afraid of tragedy and death, of
being cut off from the living and left alone, but God turns
even these places of darkness into redemption.

Jonah 1:1—2:2,11
Jonah 2:3,4,5,8
Luke 10:25–37

OCTOBER 10

You are anxious and worried about many things.
—LUKE 10:41

Some have dubbed our current era after W. H. Auden's poem "The Age of Anxiety," and today we often consider ourselves to be more anxious than those who came before us. I'm not sure we are, but our present anxiety stems from a new perspective. "We have adopted this very small view of ourselves and others," wrote Marilynne Robinson in her essay "Facing Reality," "as consumers and patients and members of interest groups, creatures too small, we may somehow hope, for great death to pause over us." We see ourselves in terms of statistics and we hope, biting our nails, that our own luck holds. "This being human—people have loved it through plague and famine and siege," Robinson goes on. "And Dante, who knew the world about suffering, had a place in hell for people who were grave when they might have rejoiced." So today, take the better part and rejoice.

Jonah 3:1–10
Psalm 130:1b–2,3–4ab,7–8
Luke 10:38–42

Wednesday

OCTOBER 11

• ST. JOHN XXIII, POPE •

Lord, teach us to pray.
—LUKE 11:1

The disciples were devout Jews; they already knew how to pray, and yet they asked Jesus, "Lord, teach us to pray." We can learn from their humble question, for no matter how long we've been trying to pray and going to Mass, we can still ask, "Teach us to pray." When I ask that question, I'm not really asking which words to use but more how to even begin, how to overcome my doubt and self-consciousness and past failures, so that I can simply sit alone and wait for the Lord. And if prayer still seems impossible, I remember what the Baptist preacher C. H. Spurgeon once said, "True prayer is measured by weight, not by length. A single groan before God may have more fullness of prayer in it than a fine oration."

Jonah 4:1–11
Psalm 86:3–4,5–6,9–10
Luke 11:1–4

Thursday

OCTOBER 12

The day that is coming will set them on fire.
—MALACHI 3:19

I often think of how eternity will bring a sudden openness of all that I've ever thought about others and all that others have thought about me. The ones I love will hear my meanest, pettiest carps and insults that I've kept hidden. And I in turn will hear theirs. We will also hear each other's loves and adorations, which we might also have kept secret. In other words, our hearts will be laid bare. I imagine this experience will divide us, as Malachi says, into those who find it torture, "blazing like an oven," and those who stand willingly under this "sun of justice." Malachi gives us a double image of heat. Some will experience it as burning, he says, leaving them neither root nor branch, but others will receive this same incandescence and be healed by its rays.

Malachi 3:13–20b
Psalm 1:1–2,3,4, and 6
Luke 11:5–13

Friday

OCTOBER 13

Their like has not been from of old.
—JOEL 2:2

Growing up, I used to feel the animated presence of
everything, my stuffed animals always on the verge of
speech, my bedroom curtains flapping like the wings of some
thoughtful thing, and even the air outside calling me to
listen. The world slowly became less enchanted as childhood
receded into ancient history, but once in a while, I try to get
that old mystery back. I imagine my church after everyone
has gone: how the great harvest angels and the stained-glass
saints might suddenly come to life and whirl about the
church. If we could watch, we'd say, "Their like has not been
from of old," but of course they'd have to rush into stillness
before we came. Yet some days when I step inside it's as if
they'd just been there, worshiping, with their wings and
robes and holy eyes.

Joel 1:13–15; 2:1–2
Psalm 9:2–3,6 and 16,8–9
Luke 11:15–26

⇒ 321 ⇐

Blessed is the womb that carried you and the breasts at which
you nursed.
—LUKE 11:27

Jesus was preaching when someone from the crowd called out, "Blessed is the womb that carried you and the breasts at which you nursed." Was this an early form of Marian devotion? And should we read Jesus' response as a corrective? "Rather," he said, just as he did when Mary came looking for him, "blessed are those who hear the word of God and observe it." I like to think that Mary was part of the crowd and that Jesus was not trying to correct—he was pointing us to her in a deeper way. "What you should honor," he might have said, "is not merely her motherhood but how her acts observed the word of God." So yes, this was an example of early devotion to Mary, and it was sanctioned by her son, who also called her blessed.

Joel 4:12–21
Psalm 97:1–2,5–6,11–12
Luke 11:27–28

OCTOBER 15

• TWENTY-EIGHTH SUNDAY IN ORDINARY TIME •

The Lord GOD will wipe away
the tears from all faces.
—ISAIAH 25:8

It is easy to read this line as a personal promise. When my baby died, I imagined God coming to me in private, like a mother. And I am sure that we will experience God's consolation in this intimate way. But the promise is actually much more grand. In the Nordic myth of Baldur the Beautiful, there is a startling image of sorrow. The beloved god is slain and then every last creature, every person and animal, not to mention every stone and twig, weeps. It is this great communion of grief we should remember, for surely every person who has ever lived has wept. So the next time you weep, imagine that almost endless company weeping too. And then imagine God coming—yes, like a mother—to wipe away every single tear.

Isaiah 25:6–10a
Psalm 23:1–3a,3b–4,5,6 (6cd)
Philippians 4:12–14,19–20
Matthew 22:1–14 or 22:1–10

OCTOBER 16

Paul, a slave of Christ Jesus, called to be an Apostle and set apart for the Gospel of God . . .
—ROMANS 1:1

Today the entire reading from Romans is an opening. Before Paul even begins his letter to the Romans in earnest, he wants to recall his debt to Scripture, to the prophets, to David, to the grace of apostleship, and above all to God. These days, when we text we don't even bother to address one another; we just start right in. We've lost a sense of indebtedness, a portrait of ourselves as part of a greater whole. Of course we'd never return to such formality, but it would be nice to see ourselves not merely as lone operators but as members or beloveds or brothers, people beholden to one another and to God. A Trappist monk once sent me a short note in which he solved this problem by signing off simply, "In Him."

Romans 1:1–7
Psalm 98:1,2–3ab,3cd–4
Luke 11:29–32

I am not ashamed of the Gospel.
—ROMANS 1:16

I'm not ashamed of the Gospel, but I'm often ashamed of
speaking about God in overt language. To many, bare
religious language smacks of fundamentalism. But if we
believe the Gospel really is the Good News, what are we to
do? Today, Paul says that people worship the created world
rather than the Creator himself. And it's at least as true now;
we're so enamored of the tangible world, we forget the real
presence behind it. But Paul also says, "Even from the
beginning of creation, God's invisible attributes have been
able to be understood and perceived in what he has made."
So we need to search for a way of revealing God's presence
in this real, physical world where people live. We need to
search for fresh language that peels back the created veil and
lets a gleam come through.

Romans 1:16–25
Psalm 19:2–3,4–5
Luke 11:37–41

Let all your works give you thanks, O LORD,
and let your faithful ones bless you.
—PSALM 145:10

I once told a famous writer that I wanted to write a good book. She gasped in horror. "Don't ever say that!" she said. "You'll never write again." When I imagine St. Luke sitting down to record his Gospel or the Acts of the Apostles, I cannot imagine how he actually began, deciding on that first word. He says that he did it by working with what had already been handed down. And in some sense that is true of all our work. It rests on the inspiration and influence and help of those who came before. So begin your work by giving thanks and remembering your work isn't just yours.

2 Timothy 4:10–17b
Psalm 145:10–11,12–13,17–18
Luke 10:1–9

What occasion is there then for boasting? It is ruled out.
—ROMANS 3:27

When I was younger, I thought that when I was forty I'd have
everything worked out, and when I was eighty I'd be an
almost perfect being full of wisdom and peace. But as I watch
people age and as I get older, I realize there never comes a
time when we're done with trouble. "All have sinned and are
deprived of the glory of God," Paul says today. It makes me
ache for humanity to see us all in this same boat, young and
old, all sinners, all deprived of the glory of God. But it also
gives me hope, for we really are in the same boat and that
creates a great brotherhood. There's no occasion for
boasting. It's ruled out. Together we must love and hope and
pray all our days.

Romans 3:21–30
Psalm 130:1b–2,3–4,5–6ab
Luke 11:47–54

Whatever you have said in the darkness will be heard in the light, and what you have whispered behind closed doors will be proclaimed on the housetops.
—LUKE 12:3

This is exactly what I was talking about a few days ago (on October 12), how every secret thing will be revealed. But now we have a fuller depiction. Angels, it seems, will stand on rooftops calling out our most hurtful thoughts. Those who have known us will reel as they hear our damaging words. And we will stand there too hearing others' meanness and slander. It will be a great cacophony of hurt. But then maybe a trumpet will sound and the messages will shift from our hate to our love. And all we can do is hope that this second round will be enough, so that instead of crumpling up in shame we'll fall into each other's arms and forgive.

Romans 4:1–8
Psalm 32:1b–2,5,11
Luke 12:1–7

The Holy Spirit will teach you at that moment what you should say.
—LUKE 12:12

The Holy Spirit is often called the forgotten member of the Trinity. We have a hard time grasping what he might be, maybe a great ghost or terrible storm, so we pray instead to the Father or Son. But the name we use in prayer can change the prayer itself. So try praying with St. Augustine: *Breathe into me, Holy Spirit, that my thoughts may all be holy. Move in me, Holy Spirit, that my work, too, may be holy. Attract my heart, Holy Spirit, that I may love only what is holy. Strengthen me, Holy Spirit, that I may defend all that is holy. Protect me, Holy Spirit, that I may always be holy.* And by praying like this we learn who the Holy Spirit really is: the One who breathes, moves, attracts, strengthens, and protects.

Romans 4:13,16–18
Psalm 105:6–7,8–9,42–43
Luke 12:8–12

Sunday

OCTOBER 22

• TWENTY-NINTH SUNDAY IN ORDINARY TIME •

I have called you by your name,
giving you a title, though you knew me not.
—ISAIAH 45:4

I remember when my children were infants, it was hard for me to accept that they were no longer part of my body. Even when they were in my arms, I'd feel a longing for them, as if even that tiny separation, a thin blanket or just our skin, was too much. But the relationship at that point was all one way. I knew everything about them, and they knew nothing of me. And yet that's not quite right, because everything they knew was me, my arms, my breath, my milk, my love. And that's how it is for God, longing and nurturing and waiting for us to finally turn and see him.

Isaiah 45:1,4–6
Psalm 96:1,3,4–5,7–8,9–10 (7b)
1 Thessalonians 1:1–5b
Matthew 22:15–21

One's life does not consist of possessions.
—LUKE 12:15

Today is the feast of the swallows, *las golondrinas*. Historically these little orange-throated birds have come by the thousands in March to nest in the eaves and archways of the Mission of San Juan Capistrano in Southern California. But around October 23, the whole flock leaves. Their fleeting forms have made them a symbol for sailors' travels and for the passage of our souls to heaven. The famous song "When the Swallows Come Back to Capistrano" plays on these comings and goings: "When the swallows come back to Capistrano that's the day you promised to come back to me. When you whispered, 'Farewell,' in Capistrano 'twas the day the swallows flew out to sea." As the swallows wing away we glimpse our fate, that one day we'll have to leave everyone and everything behind. But when they return, they come like a miracle, bringing the promise of reunion.

Romans 4:20–25
Luke 1:69–70,71–72,73–75
Luke 12:13–21

OCTOBER 24

• ST. ANTHONY MARY CLARET, BISHOP •

Where sin increased, grace overflowed all the more.
—ROMANS 5:20

This line is one of the most comforting lines in all of Scripture. If we sin and grow darker ourselves, there is not a lessening of grace but a great abounding. It reminds me of a moment in Evelyn Waugh's *Brideshead Revisited*, a book about grace if ever there was one. "I've always been bad," says Julia. "Probably I shall be bad again, punished again. But the worse I am, the more I need God. I can't shut myself out from His mercy." And that's just it. We can turn away from God if we like, but our need still beckons him. There's no way to slam the door and shut ourselves out from grace. It rushes in to fill us when we're most empty.

Romans 5:12,15b,17–19,20b–21
Psalm 40:7–8a,8b–9,10,17
Luke 12:35–38

Freed from sin, you have become slaves of righteousness.
—ROMANS 6:18

We inevitably build up habits as we live. Our plastic bodies and minds bend themselves into the shapes we prepare, even through unconscious patterns. So even though we may not count a particular choice as working toward a habit, "it is being counted none the less," says the psychologist William James. "Down among the nerve cells and fibers the molecules are counting it, registering and storing it up." It's as if the seat of judgment were there in our very bodies, keeping track of our every move. And once a habit is formed, like a well-worn path, it's hard to undo, and we become slaves to our habits. So we must be careful to walk again and again in the path of righteousness, wearing down its grass till the way is smooth.

Romans 6:12–18
Psalm 124:1b–3,4–6,7–8
Luke 12:39–48

OCTOBER 26

*I have come to set the earth on fire, and how I wish it were
already blazing!*
—LUKE 12:49

It was a beautiful but also strange thing for Jesus to say. From
the time of Exodus, God had already been known as a
consuming fire, but Jesus said, "How I wish it were already
blazing," as if that fire had died down. Five hundred years
before Christ, the Greek philosopher Heraclitus wrote, "The
world always was, is and ever shall be an ever-living fire, with
measures being kindled and measures going out." It sounds
like our Doxology, and some say Heraclitus was a Christian
without knowing it, but it also suggests that the ever-living
fire isn't always raging, it's periodically dying out and being
stirred up again. Christ set the earth on fire, but we are his
body and now we are the ones who must tend the embers.

Romans 6:19–23
Psalm 1:1–2,3,4, and 6
Luke 12:49–53

You know how to interpret the appearance of the earth and the sky; why do you not know how to interpret the present time?
—LUKE 12:56

If people back then felt smug about their ability to read the sky and understand the physical world, then how much greater is our self-satisfaction? We're no longer licking our fingers and holding them up to the wind; we have barometers, hygrometers, anemometers, and pyranometers. We expertly measure atmospheric pressure, humidity, wind speed, and solar radiation. And we imagine that our tools can interpret everything. But we're at an even greater distance from the one who once declared, "No sign will be given except the sign of Jonah," the sign of one who would go down into darkness and then rise after three days. We're just as mortal as people ever were, and yet we struggle to read the one sign that could save us.

Romans 7:18–25a
Psalm 119:66,68,76,77,93,94
Luke 12:54–59

*Through him the whole structure is held together and grows into a temple
sacred in the Lord; in him you also are being built together into a
dwelling place of God in the Spirit.*
—EPHESIANS 2:21–22

The house of God will be built, Paul says at first, on the
foundation of the prophets and apostles. It makes our
Church sound like a great pyramid, teetering upside down on
its point and us scrambling about on its great, broad base. But
then he goes on to say that through Christ we are being built
together into a dwelling place for the Spirit. This second
swirling image is more like a circle, a great sphere of people
spanning the living and the dead. I love the idea that we're
being built together, that we are not yet finished and are
not alone.

Ephesians 2:19–22
Psalm 19:2–3,4–5
Luke 6:12–16

Sunday

OCTOBER 29

• THIRTIETH SUNDAY IN ORDINARY TIME •

You shall love the Lord, your God, with all your heart, with all your
soul, and with all your mind.
—MATTHEW 22:37

Once I stayed with a beautiful group of enclosed nuns who
lived in a little city cloister. I was there at the same time as a
woman who was considering joining the order. One night we
found ourselves both taking a break in the bricked-in garden.
"Today when the gate was open it looked so pretty," she said.
Then she looked at me more intently. "Sometimes you have
to give everything up. But they also say to love God with
your mind," she said. "They do say 'mind.'" And I could tell
she was thinking of her career as a psychologist. Another
nun, contemplating final vows, recently said to me, "It's so
hard to choose. There are so many beautiful ways to live."
Yes, and so many ways to love God.

Exodus 22:20–26
Psalm 18:2–3,3–4,47,51 (2)
1 Thessalonians 1:5c–10
Matthew 22:34–40

OCTOBER 30

Blessed day by day be the LORD,
who bears our burdens; God, who is our salvation.
—PSALM 68:20

Earlier in Psalm 68, the Lord is described as riding on the
heights of the ancient heavens, which makes me think of
Helen Macdonald's memoir *H Is for Hawk*. "Looking for
goshawks is like looking for grace," she writes. "It comes but
not often and you don't get to say when or how." She
hungers after these birds she's only glimpsed in the sky and
decides to train one. When she meets her hawk for the first
time, it emerges from its cage, she says, with "brilliance and
fury," like "something bright and distant." But after she's
worked with the hawk and named it Mabel, the bird becomes
something closer, more intimate, "like a protecting spirit."
Now she calls it "My little household god." It's the same
progression of God through Scripture, at first austere, riding
on the heights of the heavens, and then coming down, day
by day, to protect us.

Romans 8:12–17
Psalm 68:2 and 4, 6–7ab,20–21
Luke 13:10–17

OCTOBER 31

Who hopes for what one sees?
—ROMANS 8:24

In one of folksinger Greg Brown's songs, he wonders why people aren't thankful for every day, but in the very next line he wonders why people don't just drink their lives away. I feel this double experience of life all the time, gratitude and despair vying for my mood. I'll hold one of my children and love him or her so much I want to break, and yet I know in that same moment that it's not forever, that one day (hopefully not soon, please not soon, Lord) we'll be asked to part. This is the truth of our lives for, as Paul says today, creation was made subject to futility. And since this is what we see, we must instead hope for what we do not see. Hope allows us to live with abandon, to love beyond what is wise given our precarious situation.

Romans 8:18–25
Psalm 126:1b–2ab,2cd–3,4–5,6
Luke 13:18–21

*After this I had a vision of a great multitude, which no one could count,
from every nation, race, people, and tongue.*
—REVELATION 7:9

I thought it would be easy to look up the total number of
saints our Church honors, but it's impossible to find out.
There are estimates at best. Some say there are more than ten
thousand, but this list includes all those who came before the
official canonization process and even includes St. Guinefort,
who is venerated in France as the protector of infants but is
also a dog. And yet such a list is only a tiny sampling of the
great, uncountable multitude of known and unknown saints
we celebrate today. We ourselves are called to join their
company. "Always and everywhere," says Pope Francis, "you
can become a saint, by being receptive to the grace that is
working in us."

Revelation 7:2–4,9–14
Psalm 24:1b–2,3–4ab,5–6
1 John 3:1–3
Matthew 5:1–12a

Yet is their hope full of immortality.
—WISDOM 3:4

The first time I remember attending the Mass of All Souls'
was a few months after I had lost my daughter. Her going
forth from me had felt like utter destruction. I sat there
crying through the psalms. I listened with desperate attention
for her name read out in the list of the dead, as if trying to
catch a spark, as it says in Wisdom, darting about in the
stubble. I carried my candle cupped in my palm like it was
her soul to the back of the church and planted it in the sand.
I stood there watching it burn in that little forest of grief and
hope, and I don't believe there could have been a greater
comfort on earth than being there with all the other grieving
people, weeping for our beloved dead and each other, our
tears full of immortality.

Wisdom 3:1–9
Psalm 23:1-3a,3b-4,5,6
Romans 5:5–11 or 6:3–9
John 6:37–40
or other readings

He sends forth his command to the earth;
swiftly runs his word!
—PSALM 147:15

I recently read an article about the history of the mail route
in India. For centuries runners sprinted barefoot from one
post to the next carrying a spear and a mailbag. The routes
were dangerous, frequented by wild beasts and bandits, and
yet the mail mostly got through. I imagine it wasn't just India
but much of the ancient world that sent letters by foot. So I
wonder when the psalmist said, "Swiftly runs his word," if
that is what he was picturing: the word of God strapped on
the back of a man, and the man running swiftly over hills and
valleys, crossing streams, pursued by danger, and yet pressing
on, feeling that good weight on his back and desperate to
make it to the end.

Romans 9:1–5
Psalm 147:12–13,14–15,19–20
Luke 14:1–6

The gifts and the call of God are irrevocable.
—ROMANS 11:29

The gifts and call of God are irrevocable, which means they cannot be taken back or undone; they are beyond recall or recovery. It sounds so heavy. Would we even want such gifts or such a call? It makes me think of C. S. Lewis alone in his room in Magdalen College at Oxford University just before he converted. "Night after night," he writes, "whenever my mind lifted even for a second from my work, [I felt] the steady, unrelenting approach of Him whom I so earnestly desired not to meet." He imagines himself a prodigal son being dragged through the gates struggling, his eyes darting about looking for escape. "The compulsion of God is our liberation," he concludes. It is hard to remain an atheist, for God is always there, dogging our steps, calling us with a call he'll never take back.

Romans 11:1–2a,11–12,25–29
Psalm 94:12–13a,14–15,17–18
Luke 14:1,7–11

I have stilled and quieted
my soul like a weaned child.
Like a weaned child on its mother's lap,
so is my soul within me.
—PSALM 131:2

I often imagine that the little girl I once was still sits straight-backed and slight, inside of me. And then around us both I imagine the skin of an old woman forming. Old people's eyes are so deep because all those younger, former selves still look through their eyes. Today the image is of a child, sitting calm and alert on her mother's lap, still close to comfort but able to turn her eyes away and look out at the world. Imagine your soul like that, still and watchful inside you. The lectionary suggests this response to the psalm: "In you, Lord, I have found my peace." We are in God, it is God's lap that holds us, when we're young and when we've grown old.

Malachi 1:14b–2:2b,8–10
Psalm 131:1,2,3
1 Thessalonians 2:7b–9,13
Matthew 23:1–12

NOVEMBER 6

Who has given him anything
that he may be repaid?
—ROMANS 11:35

I once sent Billy Collins's poem "The Lanyard" to my mother. It tells the story of a piece of junk, braided strips of plastic, that he once made out of boredom at summer camp. He presented this gift to his mother, the woman who had given him life and sustenance and everything, he says, as if it were enough to clear his debt. The whole poem is a beautiful restatement of the truth that we can never repay our parents. But Jesus tells us today how to respond. "Invite the crippled, the lame, the blind," he says, "for blessed indeed will you be for their inability to repay you." It's comforting to think that those we owe are blessed by our very failure to repay them and that what we must do in return is give like they did.

Romans 11:29–36
Psalm 69:30–31,33–34,36
Luke 14:12–14

NOVEMBER 7

Love one another with mutual affection; anticipate one another in showing honor.
—ROMANS 12:10

When I was younger and believed I had all the time in the
world, I sometimes regarded new acquaintances or invitations
as burdens, things to clutter up my time, for surely these
chances would come again and there'd be other, better
people and other, better events. But as I age, I don't take the
people I know and the events that include me for granted.
For I have finally gotten old enough to understand that this is
my life and there won't be a second time around. In today's
Gospel, the people invited to the great dinner make excuses
and refuse. So the hall fills instead with the poor, the
crippled, the blind, and the lame, and with anyone, out by
the highways and hedgerows, grateful enough to accept an
invitation and not assume it will come again.

Romans 12:5–16b
Psalm 131:1bcde,2,3
Luke 14:15–24

NOVEMBER 8

He dawns through the darkness.
—PSALM 112:4

When I was in my early twenties, I backpacked around
Scotland. At my northernmost destination, I stayed at a
sheep farm. I remember waking up in the middle of the
night, checking my watch, only four o'clock, and being
shocked to see the sun outside my window blazing down on
the fields. Since I'd expected darkness, the sun seemed
unbearably bright. Later, on the Isle of Skye, I watched the
sun go down at ten at night and the sky gradually grow a
darker blue but never turn black. I'm sure the natives barely
noticed, but to me this perpetual daylight seemed like a sign.
Though we sometimes turn away from brightness, preferring
dark, the light is out there burning always, pouring through
the universe at the greatest possible speed, forever coming,
light upon light, dawning through the darkness.

Romans 13:8–10
Psalm 112:1b–2,4–5,9
Luke 14:25–33

You are God's building.
—1 CORINTHIANS 3:9

Our faith is sacramental, so we believe physical things can show us spiritual truths, our churches representing what we ourselves must become. In a longer version of today's reading, Paul says, "You are God's field, God's building," and then later adds, "Do you not know that you are the temple of God?" He doesn't just mean each of us alone, but us together.

So we have this beautiful string of associations—fields, churches, people. It recalls that scene in the book *Where the Wild Things Are* when the little boy's room gradually becomes a forest. I'm imagining something similar: a church growing wild with prairie grass and a field sprouting candles and pews; us coming together like living stones, spreading out our love wide and wild as a field. "The temple of God, which you are," says Paul, "is holy." And so we must take good care of our temples, our people, our fields.

Ezekiel 47:1–2,8–9,12
Psalm 46:2–3,5–6,8–9
1 Corinthians 3:9c–11,16–17
John 2:13–22

NOVEMBER 10

*I myself am convinced about you, my brothers and sisters, that you
yourselves are full of goodness.*
—ROMANS 15:14

A friend just told me this lovely story. She knew a woman
once who was full of love. Every time the woman gave
someone a hug, she would deeply inhale, as if breathing in
and being filled by your essence. "It was such a beautiful gift
to be held that way," my friend said. It is one of the very best
things we can do for each other, to look into each other's
eyes or just hold each other as if to say, "I am convinced
about you. That you are full of goodness."

Romans 15:14–21
Psalm 98:1,2–3ab,3cd–4
Luke 16:1–8

⇒ 349 ⇐

NOVEMBER 11

• ST. MARTIN OF TOURS, BISHOP •

Every day will I bless you.
—PSALM 145:2

Germans say that when winter weather begins, often in mid-November, "St. Martin comes riding on a white horse," which refers both to snow and to the saint. St. Martin was a soldier who famously cut away half his cloak to give to a beggar. In many countries his feast begins on the eleventh minute of the eleventh hour of the eleventh day of the eleventh month, when bonfires and lanterns light up the streets and a man rides by on horseback. This is one reason I love the liturgical year. Instead of just time passing us by in a long, indifferent line, we have a circle that sanctifies single days and even single minutes. Instead of just winter, cold and bare, we have winter coming in like a saint. And instead of just darkness, we have fires that burn like God in the night.

Romans 16:3–9,16,22–27
Psalm 145:2–3,4–5,10–11
Luke 16:9–15

NOVEMBER 12

• THIRTY-SECOND SUNDAY IN ORDINARY TIME •

Whoever watches for her at dawn shall not be disappointed,
for he shall find her sitting by his gate.
—WISDOM 6:14

As we have noticed before, the book of Wisdom presents
God as a woman. So here is the scene: You get out of bed
earlier than usual. No one else is up; the house is filled with
quiet. You walk without creaking the floor, wanting those
few moments alone. The sky through your window is lined
with dawn but the world is still shadowy. Then you
remember why you woke up early in the first place. You
wanted to see if you cleared away all the noise and
distraction you could more easily find God. Holding your
breath, you turn and look. And there she is, sitting up against
the gate, ancient and still, as if she'd been there always,
waiting for you to find her.

Wisdom 6:12–16
Psalm 63:2,3–4,5–6,7–8 (2b)
1 Thessalonians 4:13–18 or 4:13–14
Matthew 25:1–13

God is the witness of [a man's] inmost self
and the sure observer of his heart
and the listener to his tongue.
—WISDOM 1:6

Ever since I was little, I've been hyperconscious of what everyone around me is thinking. It's a gift in some ways, for I am sensitive to how others feel, but it's also a burden, for it's hard to act when I'm perpetually aware of an external gaze. I've often said to my mother, "I wish I could find a way to reel my thoughts back inside my own head." Today we are reminded that there is only one observer who matters, the "kindly spirit" of wisdom, also referred to in this passage as the Holy Spirit and God. It helps me to focus on this inmost witness, this sure observer of my heart, this kindly spirit who anchors my thoughts within.

Wisdom 1:1–7
Psalm 139:1b–3,4–6,7–8,9–10
Luke 17:1–6

NOVEMBER 14

God formed man to be imperishable;
the image of his own nature he made them.
—WISDOM 2:23

Today the passage from Wisdom portrays death as an illusion. Those who have passed away, Wisdom tells us, may appear in the view of the foolish to be dead, but this will not be true; they will be at peace. What is actually true, the passage states again and again, is that God is crafting us: forming us, holding us like gold in the furnace to prove us, and taking us to himself. We are here now in the midst of trials and tests, being made and proved, seeing if our hope will hold, but all the while we should keep in mind that our souls, as Wisdom says, "are in the hand of God."

Wisdom 2:23–3:9
Psalm 34:2–3,16–17,18–19
Luke 17:7–10

Desire therefore my words;
long for them and you shall be instructed.
—WISDOM 6:11

We cannot learn unless we desire to learn. If we open a book
and read it only with the thought that we should learn, the
words will be nothing more than a commentary. We can
memorize the words if we wish, but they will reveal nothing,
there will be no disclosure, and we will not be instructed. In
Wallace Stevens's poem "The House Was Quiet and the
World Was Calm," he imagines a reader sitting down with a
book, leaning late over it, wanting it, the house and the quiet
becoming part of the meaning and the reader's mind. He says
the words came "as if there was no book." The poem could
almost be titled *Lectio Divina*, or "spiritual reading," for within
such calm and such desire, the book becomes a living thing.

Wisdom 6:1–11
Psalm 82:3–4,6–7
Luke 17:11–19

NOVEMBER 16

Wisdom is a spirit
intelligent, holy, unique,
Manifold, subtle, agile.
—WISDOM 7:22B

I get stuck sometimes in prayer trying to imagine the *how* of God. How does God come to me? How does he dwell within? Today in the book of Wisdom, Solomon gives us a little treatise on the how of God. At first, it might not seem as if Solomon is talking about God at all, for he personifies wisdom as a woman. But repeatedly she's given the attributes of God himself, of Christ and the Spirit. So how does she come? She's pure and very subtle, mobile beyond all motion, an aura of the might of God, the refulgence of eternal light, and passes into holy souls from age to age. It helps my imagination. Just by picking a few of the adjectives offered today, I can better imagine that keen, unhampered, kindly one coming to me.

Wisdom 7:22b–8:1
Psalm 119:89,90,91,130,135,175
Luke 17:20–25

*From the greatness and the beauty of created things
their original author, by analogy, is seen.*
—WISDOM 13:5

I remember being out on the deck of some ferryboat late at night, my family back in the lighted cabin. Positioned between the ones I love and the moon shining across the water, I suddenly felt an ache. It seemed to point to something behind or beneath everything around me, as if a great spirit stood there holding it all forth. And the ache, far from unpleasant, gave me the sense that I could die right then and there and be satisfied. In the circuit of stars and mighty water, we should be able to see, claims Wisdom, that an "original source of beauty fashioned them." I was not a believer back then, so I should ask myself the question that ends our reading: How did I not more quickly find the Lord?

Wisdom 13:1–9
Psalm 19:2–3,4–5ab
Luke 17:26–37

He still reached to heaven, while he stood upon the earth.
—WISDOM 18:16

Writers often look at an object or a person and then look again from a different angle. The shifting perspective can help flesh out the description, lift it off the page into life.

Often, I think, my faith suffers from a singleness of perspective. I picture Jesus, the man, who lived long ago and died, and I fail to look from other angles. Today we're given a new perspective. First the scene is set: "When peaceful stillness compassed everything and the night in its swift course was half-spent." It's as if we are peering through a window into the gloom when a great figure, like a statue come to life, walks by. "He still reached to heaven," says the Book of Wisdom, "while he stood upon the earth." And we see anew the one who was both man and God.

Wisdom 18:14–16; 19:6–9
Psalm 105:2–3,36–37,42–43
Luke 18:1–8

Sunday

NOVEMBER 19

• THIRTY-THIRD SUNDAY IN ORDINARY TIME •

She puts her hands to the distaff,
and her fingers ply the spindle.
—PROVERBS 31:19–20

This image is an old-fashioned portrait of womanhood, but it
presents an image not of subservience but of power and skill.
"She girds herself with strength; / she exerts her arms with
vigor," it says later on in Proverbs. "She is clothed with
strength and dignity, / and laughs at the days to come."
Lately I've been longing for a more physical life, to see the
actual work of my hands. Modern life is so abstract, cut off
from things and persons, many of us hiding behind our desks
in offices and houses, our work scrolling by on a screen. We
can't roll back time, and such a life would no doubt have its
own frustrations and lacks, but we can strive in our own lives
for strength and vigor and the ability to laugh at the days
to come.

Proverbs 31:10–13,19–20,30–31
Psalm 128:1–2,3,4–5
1 Thessalonians 5:1–6
Matthew 25:14–30 or 25:14–15,19–21

⇒ 358 ⇐

NOVEMBER 20

Jesus of Nazareth is passing by.
—LUKE 18:37

On Saturday we saw Jesus from the angle of mythic grandeur, a great figure stretching up to heaven even as he stood on earth. This passage from Luke gives us another angle. Instead of peering through a nighttime window at the strange goings-on of God, we look through the eyes of a blind man. He's seated beside the roadside as a crowd approaches. Someone says, "Jesus of Nazareth is passing by." The blind man cannot see him but imagines this figure foretold by the prophets. "Son of David," he cries out, "have pity on me." Then he feels Jesus stop and stand before him, an almost tangible presence of compassion and goodness. "Lord, please let me see," he says. "Have sight," Jesus says. "Your faith has saved you." It may save us, too, for through his blind eyes our vision clears a little more.

1 Maccabees 1:10–15,41–43,54–57,62–63
Psalm 119:53,61,134,150,155,158
Luke 18:35–43

I will prove myself worthy of my old age.
—2 MACCABEES 6:27

This startling story tells of the execution of a very old man, Eleazar. When faced with torture and death, he makes up his mind, it says, "in a noble manner, worthy of his years, the dignity of his advanced age, the merited distinction of his gray hair," to be loyal to the holy laws given by God. Right before he dies, Eleazar says that even though his body is enduring terrible pain, he is also suffering it with joy in his soul. Not only is this a beautiful portrayal of death without fear, but it makes old age something not to dread, but to aspire to. Imagine if we watched our skin grow wrinkled as if it were our dignity and our hair turn gray as if it were a coming crown.

2 Maccabees 6:18–31
Psalm 3:2–3,4–5,6–7
Luke 19:1–10

Keep me as the apple of your eye.
—PSALM 17:8

I was surprised to see this saying we use today in a psalm, so I looked it up and found that the original Hebrew is translated more literally as "the little man of your eye." It's a reference to the miniature reflection you can see of yourself in another person's eye. The word *pupil*, in fact, is quite similar, for it means a little doll or little boy or girl, referring again to "the small reflected image seen when looking into someone's pupil." This leads, also, to the sense of pupil as a schoolchild. With this translation of the Hebrew, we can see ourselves held within God's gaze, his children, tiny figures moving about within his all-seeing eyes.

2 Maccabees 7:1,20–31
Psalm 17:1bcd,5–6,8b and 15
Luke 19:11–28

NOVEMBER 23

As Jesus drew near Jerusalem, he saw the city and wept over it.
—LUKE 19:41

In the Old Testament, we often hear of God's fury, his desire to crush the sinful and bring justice. Against this image, the psalms continually assert God's compassion, as if not quite convinced. He is slow to anger, the psalms say. Isn't he? He is filled with kindness, Oh we pray. But Jesus brings us the true face of God, and we don't have to guess anymore. What we see is not anger but the hope of Scripture: a face full of tears. Today I give thanks for many things, but above all for a God who weeps.

1 Maccabees 2:15–29
Psalm 50:1b–2,5–6,14–15
Luke 19:41–44

Friday

NOVEMBER 24

• ST. ANDREW DŨNG-LAC, PRIEST, AND COMPANIONS, MARTYRS •

All the people were hanging on his words.
—LUKE 19:48

Translating even more literally from the Greek translation, the line reads, "They hung upon him hearing." And we get the sense of a double suspension: people hanging on his arms and knees, draped there, clinging for dear life, but also people hanging upon his words, clutching each one to hear it better. In this passage it was precisely how closely the people gathered around him and how intently they listened that kept the chief priests from finding a way to "accomplish their purpose" and put him to death. It's a radical thought, that we can forestall calamity by closing in on the Word. Could we ever get close enough? Would there ever be enough of us to matter? And yet that is our hope. So let us hang upon him hearing, as his followers once did.

1 Maccabees 4:3–37,52–59
1 Chronicles 29:10bcd,11abc,11d–12a,12bcd
Luke 19:45–48

———————

He is not God of the dead, but of the living, for to him all are alive.
—LUKE 20:38

We have a terror of the undead, or "the living dead," as they are often called thanks to George Romero's movie *Night of the Living Dead*. The horror writer W. B. Seabrook describes the undead like this: "They were in truth like the eyes of a dead man, not blind, but staring, unfocused, unseeing. The whole face, for that matter, was bad enough. It was vacant, as if there were nothing behind it." In Colm Tóibín's novel *The Testament of Mary*, he describes the risen Lazarus in a similar way: ghoulish, blank, miserable, unable to eat. This imagined fate of Lazarus seems worse than death, more than an end of life, a negation. But all of this is a world without God, without the one who sees every last soul, here and beyond, in its bright beauty, and never stops calling each one to arise.

1 Maccabees 6:1–13
Psalm 9:2–3,4 and 6,16 and 19
Luke 20:27–40

NOVEMBER 26

• OUR LORD JESUS CHRIST, KING OF THE UNIVERSE •

The LORD is my shepherd; I shall not want.
In verdant pastures he gives me repose.
—PSALM 23:1

In the lectionary, today is titled "The Last Sunday in Ordinary Time." I can't help reading this as the last Sunday marking commonplace, everyday life. And yet I know that's not true. Underneath our liturgical calendar that moves in a circle our own days run, trucking along, always moving forward and usually quite emphatically ordinary. So it is reassuring to hear on this day in particular that we have a shepherd who guides us on the right paths and who refreshes our souls. "I will rescue them from every place where they were scattered when it was cloudy and dark," God says in Ezekiel. And again we have that image of God coming through the fog to find us, even on these commonplace, everyday roads.

Ezekiel 34:11–12,15–17
Psalm 23:1–2,2–3,5–6 (1)
1 Corinthians 15:20–26,28
Matthew 25:31–46

⇒ 365 ⇐

NOVEMBER 27

But she, from her poverty, has offered her whole livelihood.
—LUKE 21:4

It's not difficult to give from our abundance. When I had an
infant in my arms and felt overflowing love, I would smile
more readily at strangers, almost as if I thought my happiness
would spill over onto them. It wasn't conscious, but I
remember it now when I see that same expression of general
benevolence on the faces of new mothers. In some ways it's a
beautiful thing, spreading joy around, but when things are
good, this kind of generosity is easy to achieve. Earlier, when
my arms were empty and my first baby buried, did I look at
anyone that way? Did I look at anyone at all? Or was my face
turned away in bitterness? "This poor widow put in more
than all the rest," Jesus says. The widow put in more, because
she gave not from abundance but from poverty.

Daniel 1:1–6,8–20
Daniel 3:52,53,54,55,56
Luke 21:1–4

NOVEMBER 28

The stone that struck the statue became a great mountain and filled the whole earth.
—DANIEL 2:35

Lately, in the daily readings we've been collecting ways of seeing Jesus. Here is one more. Throughout Scripture, he's referred to as a rock. The stone the builders rejected. A stone to strike and a rock to stumble over. A cornerstone for the foundation. A spiritual rock from which to drink. Today we see him by way of a great stone, a figure hewn from a mountain, smashing down its cliff, shattering everything false, and then growing, filling the earth, forming the very ground under our feet.

Daniel 2:31–45
Daniel 3:57,58,59,60,61
Luke 21:5–11

NOVEMBER 29

*Suddenly, opposite the lampstand, the fingers of a human hand appeared,
writing on the plaster of the wall in the king's palace.*
—DANIEL 5:5

Today's passage presents a chilling scene. The king and his
company are drinking and feasting, praising the gods of gold
and silver, bronze and iron, wood and stone, when a ghostly
hand appears. It proceeds to write a riddle on the wall that
foretells the fall of the kingdom. The expression "the writing
on the wall" comes from this ancient banquet. We use it even
in trivial situations to mean that something is about to
happen. But the truly chilling moment is when Daniel says,
"The God in whose hand is your life breath and the whole
course of your life, you did not glorify." If we look closely
enough, this is the writing on every wall. This is the warning
we must heed.

Daniel 5:1–6,13–14,16–17,23–28
Daniel 3:62,63,64,65,66,67
Luke 21:12–19

NOVEMBER 30

• ST. ANDREW, APOSTLE •

As it is written, How beautiful are the feet of those who bring
the good news!
—ROMANS 10:15

There is no Ash Wednesday for Advent, no day before the
first Sunday to let us know what's coming. But the readings
today, on the feast of St. Andrew, have that feel. They echo
the prophets. "How beautiful upon the mountains are the feet
of the one bringing good news!" Isaiah once cried. "At this
moment on the mountains," cried Nahum, "the footsteps of
one announcing peace!" *Shhhh.* Listen. Can you hear them
drawing near, the distant footfalls of the prophets, the
apostles, the martyrs, and the saints? They are coming,
bearing good news, bringing tidings of peace. It's all about to
begin. How beautiful are their feet!

Romans 10:9–18
Psalm 19:8,9,10,11
Matthew 4:18–22

Friday

DECEMBER 1

*Thrones were set up
and the Ancient One took his throne.
His clothing was snow bright,
and the hair on his head as white as wool.*
—DANIEL 7:9

Here we have another image not of Jesus, but of God the
Father sitting on his throne. Scholars interpret this as a
portrait of ongoing preparation for the Apocalypse. But
reading this today, so close to Advent, I get a different sense.
God is seated there in the midst of fire, called Ancient of
Days, as some translations say. Concentric circles of angels,
like flocking birds or butterflies, move about him, but he is
alone, for the book is open. The Word has been sent out into
the world; the Incarnation is at hand. I like to think of him
sitting there in solitude, mirroring the experience of his Son,
God torn from God, allowing himself, unbelievably, to enter
our loneliness.

Daniel 7:2–14
Daniel 3:75,76,77,78,79,80,81
Luke 21:29–33

⇒ 370 ⇐

DECEMBER 2

You sons of men, bless the Lord;
praise and exalt him above all forever.
—DANIEL 3:87

We've been singing this song for many days. It's often called
the "Canticle of Three Children," for it was sung by three
young men who were cast into a furnace for refusing to
worship a golden idol. They were about to die, the fire
mounting about them; it was the end. And then a radiant
figure appeared and turned the fire into breeze and dew. The
children of God began to sing, calling out to every part of
creation. "You sons of men," they cry today, including us in
their song, "bless the Lord." And today on the eve of Advent,
it is also our end, the end of our year. But a radiant figure is
coming for us too, and tomorrow what looked like an end
will turn once more into a beginning.

Daniel 7:15–27
Daniel 3:82–83,84,85,86,87
Luke 21:34–36

DECEMBER 3

• FIRST SUNDAY OF ADVENT •

Oh, that you would rend the heavens and come down,
with the mountains quaking before you.
—ISAIAH 63:19B

We begin Advent with this call for God to come down. "Stir up your power and come to save us," the psalm also cries. But the New Testament readings are more sober. "May he not come suddenly and find you sleeping," warns Mark. Paul tries to reassure us that God will keep us firm and that we will in fact be able to stand on the irreproachable day of our Lord. Even Isaiah pictures the mountains quaking. The poet and painter William Blake was once asked how he managed to begin the awesome task of illustrating Dante's *Divine Comedy*. He answered, "With fear and trembling." We are standing at the beginning, calling up to heaven for God to come down. If we aren't quaking like the mountains, we should be.

Isaiah 63:16b–17,19b; 64:2–7
Psalm 80:2–3,15–16,18–19 (4)
1 Corinthians 1:3–9
Mark 13:33–37

We will go up to the house of the LORD.
—PSALM 122:1

In this season we usually imagine that it is we who must wait
for God to come. But today the readings point out a different
possibility. The psalm imagines the tribes of Israel going up
to give thanks to the Lord. Isaiah says that all nations shall
stream toward the Lord's house. And even in Matthew the
centurion has sought out Jesus, not the other way around. To
put this idea into practice, try this Advent tradition: instead
of placing the wise men next to your Nativity scene, put
them somewhere else in your house, and day by day move
them closer. The meeting at Christmas involves two arrivals.
God must come, yes, but we must come too. So let us go to
the house of the Lord. Let us stream toward it.

Isaiah 2:1–5
Psalm 122:1–2,3–4b,4cd–5,6–7,8–9
Matthew 8:5–11

DECEMBER 5

*A shoot shall sprout from the stump of Jesse,
and from his roots a bud shall blossom.*
—ISAIAH 11:1

God doesn't come as we might expect. That ancient man on
the throne encircled by angels doesn't just step down into
our world and lay the mountains low, bringing all his glory
and fanfare with him. Instead a tiny shoot sprouts up, a bud,
a little baby who doesn't yet know how to talk. We are
standing here trembling, waiting for the hour to come, but
we will see not a warrior or king, but this helpless child, God
dwindled down into a little body and downy head, the
creator of the universe laid in our arms, and we will be
undone. We will look down like a new mother, astonished
and in love, trembling still, and pray that we will be able to
guard this new life and let it grow.

Isaiah 11:1–10
Psalm 72:1–2,7–8,12–13,17
Luke 10:21–24

Where could we ever get enough bread in this deserted place to satisfy such a crowd?
—MATTHEW 15:33

Today the readings are all about feasting. In Advent, as in Lent, we are meant to fast and be somber and wait. But there are a few days that break through this quietness and announce the coming joy. And it seems fitting on the feast of St. Nicholas, when that old saint is said to fill children's shoes and stockings with chocolate and marzipan and gold. In our house, we tell our children that Santa Claus is real—and we hope that they will someday forgive us for being the ones to carry out his benevolent will. We hope that they will see that this is how it works. For these days, in this deserted place, it's we who must distribute the loaves and fishes. We must prepare the feast.

Isaiah 25:6–10a
Psalm 23:1–3a,3b–4,5,6
Matthew 15:29–37

Thursday

DECEMBER 7

• ST. AMBROSE, BISHOP AND DOCTOR OF THE CHURCH •

This gate is the LORD's.
—PSALM 118:20

Today we hear about gates. "Open up the gates to let in a nation!" cries Isaiah. "Open to me the gates of justice!" says the psalm. But Jesus warns, "Not everyone who says to me, 'Lord, Lord,' will enter the Kingdom of heaven, but only the one who does the will of my Father." These are upsetting words, but we should read them in context. Just moments earlier Jesus said, "Knock and the door will be opened to you." So it seems that knocking is doing God's will, while merely calling out "Lord" is not enough. Calling out requires little effort, but to knock on a door we must first seek it out. So let us join Isaiah and the psalmist who went in search of the gate. The gate is the Lord's and only he can open it, but first we must knock.

Isaiah 26:1–6
Psalm 118:1 and 8–9,19–21,25–27a
Matthew 7:21,24–27

*The man called his wife Eve, because she became the mother of all
the living.*
—GENESIS 3:20

She brought death into the world, and yet she was called
Eve—*Hawah* in Hebrew, which means "to live." It is a name
full of hope. Evolutionary biologists estimate that there have
been 7,500 generations since the beginning of humanity. As
we move farther back in our own family trees, other trees
join ours, until the entire human race is beneath a single
woman. I picture that original woman looking out on her
progeny filling the earth and finding herself not the mother
of the living but of the dead. And yet there is one, a distant
daughter, who walks toward her. "Through me your name has
been redeemed," says the daughter. And it is true, for we call
this daughter *Mater Viventium*, mother of the living. In her,
Mary, the hope of Eve is fulfilled.

Genesis 3:9–15,20
Psalm 98:1,2–3ab,3cd–4
Ephesians 1:3–6,11–12
Luke 1:26–38

DECEMBER 9

• ST. JUAN DIEGO CUAUHTLATOATZIN •

No longer will your Teacher hide himself,
but with your own eyes you shall see your Teacher.
While from behind, a voice shall sound in your ears:
"This is the way; walk in it."
—ISAIAH 30:21

The path of faith is not a line but a circle. We are back at the
beginning of this path. We no longer have our Teacher in
sight. He is hidden. And yet, the entire liturgical year we just
walked through is behind us, like a gentle hand on our back.
"This is the way," comes a voice out of all that Scripture;
"walk in it." So we continue on in the dark of December,
heading toward the moment when our Teacher will
appear again.

Isaiah 30:19–21,23–26
Psalm 147:1–2,3–4,5–6
Matthew 9:35–10:1,5a,6–8

In the desert prepare the way of the LORD!
—ISAIAH 40:3

The Werner Herzog film *Grizzly Man* documents the life of a
young dreamer who must have imagined he was living in
Eden, for every summer he flew to a remote Alaskan reserve
to live with the grizzly bears, which eventually killed him.
"What haunts me," says Herzog, "is that in all the faces of all
the bears that Treadwell ever filmed, I discover no kinship,
no understanding, no mercy. I see only the overwhelming
indifference of nature." Nature is indifferent and can claim
our lives, but in a sense we like it that way, for it shows us a
world beyond ourselves, a world we didn't make and don't
control, a world in which we might discover the presence
of God.

Isaiah 40:1–5,9–11
Psalm 85:9–10,11–12,13–14 (8)
2 Peter 3:8–14
Mark 1:1–8

DECEMBER 11

A highway will be there,
called the holy way.
—ISAIAH 35:8

And a bit later Isaiah adds, "It is for those with a journey to make." *Holy way* is another name for pilgrimage. The poet Anne Carson, who writes about pilgrimage, says this, "Since ancient times pilgrimages have been conducted from place to place, in the belief that a question can travel into an answer." We are those with a journey to make. We are headed out on the highway, full of questions. Ahead an answer waits, greater than any question could ever guess.

Isaiah 35:1–10
Psalm 85:9ab and 10,11–12,13–14
Luke 5:17–26

Tuesday

DECEMBER 12

• OUR LADY OF GUADALUPE •

A great sign appeared in the sky, a woman clothed with the sun, with the moon under her feet, and on her head a crown of twelve stars.
—REVELATION 12:1

Our Lady of Guadalupe stands in front of the sun, a cloak of stars falling about her and a crescent moon under her feet. In our church, her painted statue faces a shrine for St. Anthony of Padua, who holds forth the Christ child. It's as if they're both in the grotto. St. Anthony looks searchingly at Mary, unable to believe what he's been allowed to touch. And she looks down at them as if with a nod. It's why we, too, so often look to her. She softens divinity, cloaking its stars, standing in front of its light so we're not blinded, nodding us on day by day as we get closer to the manger.

Zechariah 2:14–17 or
Revelation 11:19a; 12:1–6a,10ab
Judith 13:18bcde,19
Luke 1:26–38 or 1:39–47

⇒ 381 ⇐

Bless the LORD, O my soul.
—PSALM 103:1

We are approaching the "O Antiphon" sequence of Advent. An antiphon is literally a returned sound, a song sung in response to another song. They are called "O Antiphons" because each one begins with a short emotional note of wonder. From December 17 to December 23, we begin each day with a new name of Jesus, producing this litany: "O Wisdom, O Lord, O Root of Jesse, O Key of David, O Dayspring, O King of the Nations, O Emmanuel." But today, as if preparing ourselves for that great song, we talk instead to our own souls. Now the O is pleading. "O my soul," we say, hoping we'll manage it. "Bless the Lord." And this song of our soul goes out to meet that song, that antiphon, that's been coming in response, coming ever since before creation.

Isaiah 40:25–31
Psalm 103:1–2,3–4,8 and 10
Matthew 11:28–30

DECEMBER 14

I will make of you a threshing sledge,
sharp, new, and double-edged.
—ISAIAH 41:15

Those of us who live in cities today have lost any visceral relationship to threshing, a practice in which grain is separated from the plant. It happens far away, in some great field, by some whirring machine that doesn't concern us. But people used to trample the grain with their own feet or beat it with flails. Threshing was physical. Now we use our bodies for so little. Even the women I once saw in India brushing grain onto the road were using the weight of passing cars to separate their wheat. But here God says that he will make us into a threshing hammer with a double edge. "I believe God made me for a purpose," says a character in the film *Chariots of Fire*, "but he also made me fast. And when I run I feel His pleasure." It might be a good corrective to engage our bodies sometimes, to feel ourselves grow strong and powerful in pursuit of God's pleasure.

Isaiah 41:13–20
Psalm 145:1 and 9,10–11,12–13ab
Matthew 11:11–15

DECEMBER 15

To what shall I compare this generation? It is like children who sit in marketplaces and call to one another.
—MATTHEW 11:16

Children have always been children, playing in the streets. Here they taunt each other with songs and tunes on the flute, each ditty intended to produce a response. "I played, but you didn't dance," one child teased. "I sang, but you didn't cry." When children play, they play at reality, trying out grief and joy before these things become real. Play is the work of childhood. If we play and explore as children, psychologists say, we're better able to deal with reality as adults. But it's a lifelong struggle to confront reality, to dance when we're called to dance and cry when we're called to cry.

Isaiah 48:17–19
Psalm 1:1–2,3,4 and 6
Matthew 11:16–19

I tell you that Elijah has already come.
—MATTHEW 17:11

This passage ends by confirming that Jesus is speaking of John the Baptist. It's the closest Scripture comes to reincarnation. But another passage says that John will come in the spirit and power of Elijah, not as Elijah himself. Once a yoga teacher asked me if I thought souls could be reincarnated as trees. I said, "No, do you?" "I know they can," she said. I walked away annoyed. My theology seemed, right then, to be less open to life. But hers seemed glib, as if any fluttering thing might have a soul. I should have been more generous, though, for belief in reincarnation is just the desire to see someone or something again and be interconnected. Christians desire this too, but we believe the spirit of God will animate all things and unite us; we'll be one body but still ourselves.

Sirach 48:1–4,9–11
Psalm 80:2ac and 3b,15–16,18–19
Matthew 17:9a,10–13

Sunday

DECEMBER 17

• THIRD SUNDAY OF ADVENT •

*There is one among you whom you do not recognize, the one who is
coming after me.*
—JOHN 1:26–27

Today John the Baptist asserts his belief in Jesus, the one who
is coming. But later in prison his belief will falter and he'll
ask, is Jesus "the one who is to come?" (Matthew 11:3 NAB).
  This makes me think of a story a friend once told me.
Growing up, she had a mentor who was her pillar of faith.
But when this mentor grew old, he asked his visitors, "Do
you think it's all true?" My friend was crestfallen, alarmed that
the one who'd always been sure really wasn't. Maybe it would
have helped her to hear that John the Baptist had similar
doubt. He'd once proclaimed that Jesus was the Messiah, but
now he wanted someone else to carry that conviction. We do
not hold faith alone. We trade it back and forth, carrying it
for each other.

Isaiah 61:1–2a,10–11
Luke 1:46–48,49–50,53–54 (Isaiah 61:10b)
1 Thessalonians 5:16–24
John 1:6–8,19–28

She will bear a son and you are to name him Jesus, because he will save his people from their sins.
—MATTHEW 1:21

The angel could have told Joseph any name in the world and he would have given it to his son. But the angel of the Lord told him Jesus. He probably used the original Hebrew *Yehoshua* or *Yeshua* instead. Etymologists suggest a translation for the name as "God saves" or "God is a saving cry" or "God is my help," so the *Catechism* notes that the very name of God is present in the name of his Son. And I like thinking that when I say his name, I'm not just saying a noun, referring to a static person who lived long ago, but a noun followed by a verb. I'm not just saying the name Jesus; I am making a claim: "God saves; God is my help."

Jeremiah 23:5–8
Psalm 72:1–2,12–13,18–19
Matthew 1:18–25

DECEMBER 19

Though you are barren and have had no children, yet you will conceive and bear a son.
—JUDGES 13:3

This line from the reading by itself does not make clear which barren woman of the Bible is receiving this message. Is it Sarah or Rebecca or Hannah or Elizabeth? In this case, it's an unnamed woman who stands before what she calls a terrible angel and does "not ask him where he came from." *Barren* is taken from a root that means "like a man," sterile or bare. But it also can be applied to anything to mean fruitless, unproductive, dull. So these scenes between women and angels speak to all of us, male and female, to all our endeavors. God does not want our work to come to nothing, our lives to be bare. But be warned, if you pray for transformation, it might come out of nowhere and stand terrible before you and you will never be the same again.

Judges 13:2–7,24–25a
Psalm 71:3–4a,5–6ab,16–17
Luke 1:5–25

DECEMBER 20

But Mary said to the angel, "How can this be, since I have no relations with a man?"
—LUKE 1:34

Just yesterday in Luke, when Zechariah asked, "How shall I know this?" Gabriel chastised him, saying, "Now you will be speechless and unable to talk . . . because you did not believe my words." But here when Mary asks that same question, the angel kneels, trying not to scare her, and explains. Up to now, infertile women had suddenly been able to conceive with their husbands and bear a son, but Mary conceived a son, produced a Y chromosome when her body carried none, without ever having been with a man. It is the one supernatural conception in Scripture. Every other birth had been unlikely, but this one was impossible. It deserved a question.

Isaiah 7:10–14
Psalm 24:1–2,3–4ab,5–6
Luke 1:26–38

Thursday

DECEMBER 21

• ST. PETER CANISIUS, PRIEST AND DOCTOR OF THE CHURCH •

> *Here he stands behind our wall,*
> *gazing through the windows,*
> *peering through the lattices.*
> —SONG OF SONGS 2:9

It's supposed to be the lover in Song of Songs who prowls about the walls and peers in. But it's a slightly creepy image. One of the scariest scenes in horror movies is when a dark window suddenly fills up with a face. At night we cannot see out our windows. We cannot see what sees us. So when a face suddenly gets close enough that our inside light illuminates it, it's too late. Whatever was coming is here, upon us, and we cannot get away. But maybe that is exactly how it is as God closes in. He is out there, sure enough, circling the walls of our lives, gazing in at us. But we see through a glass darkly and do not notice until it's too late and we cannot get away.

Song of Songs 2:8–14 or Zephaniah 3:14–18a
Psalm 33:2–3,11–12,20–21
Luke 1:39–45

⇒ 390 ⇐

I prayed for this child, and the LORD granted my request. Now I, in turn, give him to the LORD.
—1 SAMUEL 1:27

It reminds me of the bargain made in so many fairy tales. A wish is granted by an old witch, but only on the condition that a firstborn child is given up. How would it change things if when we prayed we realized that that's the deal? What we pray for is never meant to be kept but given away. Our gifts, such as they are, and even our children are things we must eventually yield. We must be able to stand like Hannah and say, "He shall be dedicated to the Lord." But remember, it is not an old witch who asks this of us but the one who seeks out what has gone by, gathers up all things, and someday gives them back.

1 Samuel 1:24–28
1 Samuel 2:1,4–5,6–7,8abcd
Luke 1:46–56

All who heard these things took them to heart, saying, "What, then, will this child be?"
—LUKE 1:66

It's the question every parent asks: "What, then, will this child be?" Sometimes it's asked in despair, sometimes in pride. But both of these attitudes are the wrong way to look at a child. Teacher and writer Susan Schaeffer Macaulay asks us to perform this experiment. "Take a small child on your knee," she says. "Do not see him as something to prune, form, or mold. . . . He is a separate human being whose strength lies in who he is, not in who he will become. . . . You are holding a *person* on your knee." This perspective ends all that striving that weighs down modern parents. After all, we're called to become not some winner of awards but a person, like that very child on our knee.

Malachi 3:1–4,23–24
Psalm 25:4–5ab,8–9,10 and 14
Luke 1:57–66

Sunday

DECEMBER 24

· FOURTH SUNDAY OF ADVENT ·

In heaven you have confirmed your faithfulness.
—PSALM 89:3

This communal psalm is a plea for this to be true, for God to
be faithful and save us. Later in this psalm, in order to shore
themselves up, the community recalls God's power: "Yours
are the heavens," they cry, "yours the earth." Once this same
cry was in my mind. I was kneeling at my daughter's grave,
just a year after losing her, remembering her body being
lowered into the earth, how I wanted to stay there on the
fresh grass and never leave. On this return visit, with a new
baby in my arms, I could still feel the tug of the earth on my
heart. Just then two bald eagles, rare in those parts, soared
into the sky over the clearing. I stood there between the
eagles and the grave, praying some wordless version of
Yours are the heavens, Lord, yours the earth.

2 Samuel 7:1–5,8b–12,14a,16
Psalm 89:2–3,4–5,27,29 (2a)
Romans 16:25–27
Luke 1:26–38

DECEMBER 25

Let us go, then, to Bethlehem to see this thing that has taken place.
—LUKE 2:15

I teach a calculus class once a week to college students. I try to help them master the techniques, but also give them some sense of the surprise in mathematics, how when these ideas first formed in one person's mind they came as a glorious shock. But it's hard. All the ideas were discovered long ago, and now they seem derivative. "Of course, that's true," they invariably react. "It's in the book." That's also the problem with faith. It happened long ago; it's in the book. So we have to imagine ourselves back into that night when the angels came and shone around the shepherds. We must go once again to Bethlehem to see this thing that has taken place.

VIGIL:
Isaiah 62:1–5
Psalm 89:4–5,16–17,27,29 (2a)
Acts 13:16–17,22–25
Matthew 1:1–25 or 1:18–25

DAWN:
Isaiah 62:11–12
Psalm 97:1,6,11–12
Titus 3:4–7
Luke 2:15–20

NIGHT:
Isaiah 9:1–6
Psalm 96:1–2,2–3,11–12,13 (Luke 2:11)
Titus 2:11–14
Luke 2:1–14

DAY:
Isaiah 52:7–10
Psalm 98:1,2–3,3–4,5–6 (3c)
Hebrews 1:1–6
John 1:1–18 or 1:1–5,9–14

Tuesday

DECEMBER 26

• ST. STEPHEN, THE FIRST MARTYR •

Into your hands I commend my spirit;
you will redeem me, O LORD.
—PSALM 31:6

It is hard to celebrate a death, even the death of a martyr, the
day after a birth. But how many people have died on
Christmas? If you open the U.S. Census Bureau's Population
Clock online, you will see the births and deaths ticking by as
we speak. The births greatly outweigh the deaths, but for a
family or an individual who has lost a loved one, there is no
quantity of new lives that could outweigh his or her pain.
And yet there is one birth that does just that. His single life
outweighs every death that has ever been. So we must be
able to say, "Into your hands I commend my spirit or the
spirit of the one I love," and know that those hands are
strong enough to hold all our deaths and redeem each one.

Acts 6:8–10; 7:54–59
Psalm 31:3cd–4,6 and 8ab,16bc and 17
Matthew 10:17–22

Wednesday

DECEMBER 27

• ST. JOHN, APOSTLE AND EVANGELIST •

The life was made visible;
we have seen it and testify to it
and proclaim to you the eternal life.
—1 JOHN 1:2–3

I don't believe that Christianity is a departure from all that came before. I don't believe, in some sense, that there is anything new under the sun. And yet the birth of Jesus changed everything. Before he came, there was a great yearning expressed in the myths, in philosophy, in the words of the prophets. These voices cried out their hope that God would not abandon us to death, that there was meaning beyond life. Two days ago the life that would answer these voices was again made visible. It came not as a new thing but as a confirmation, a proclamation, that what had long been hoped for, theorized, prophesied now lay under the sun as real as you and I.

1 John 1:1–4
Psalm 97:1–2,5–6,11–12
John 20:1a and 2–8

DECEMBER 28

If we say, "We have fellowship with him," while we continue to walk in darkness, we lie and do not act in truth.
—1 JOHN 1:6

After speaking these words, in the very next breath John says, "If we say we are without sin, we deceive ourselves, and the truth is not in us." It's a tricky pair of statements. Sin is a sign that we're in darkness, and yet claiming that we're without sin is also a sign of darkness. How are we to get out of this fix? "If we acknowledge our sins," John says, "he is faithful and just and will forgive." We get out of this fix by confessing. After my very first confession, I remember the feeling of coming out of the church and light being everywhere, on the leaves, on the sidewalk, on my swinging arms. Why is it so hard for me to go back?

1 John 1:5–2:2
Psalm 124:2–3,4–5,7b–8
Matthew 2:13–18

You yourself a sword will pierce.
—LUKE 2:35

I think the prophecy from this passage could be made to any mother who holds her newly born child. With birth comes a sudden confrontation with both the incredible gift of life and its fragility. She looks down into all that innocence, a life that wouldn't have come to be if it weren't for her, and feels a fierce desire to protect it. Any suffering that comes for this child will, in some sense, be traced back to this moment, the moment when the child entered the land of the living. She knows, too, that her own happiness is now forever linked to this life, and that if anything should happen to it, she will lose part of herself as well. So even if she hadn't been a praying person before now, she feels this piercing sword in the midst of her greatest joy and begins to pray.

1 John 2:3–11
Psalm 96:1–2a,2b–3,5b–6
Luke 2:22–35

DECEMBER 30

The child grew and became strong, filled with wisdom; and the favor of God was upon him.
—LUKE 2:40

We meditate all the time on the infancy of Jesus and his final days, but what about those years when he was learning how to talk and every day was growing a little bit taller? We might imagine him as Adam, the first man, who was also surely once a boy, at home in the world, at peace with birds and animals, and comfortable walking among the trees and grasses, no enmity between him and creation. Add to that the compassion that comes from knowing and loving humanity, something that only came late to Adam. And then picture a gentleness, a wisdom, a clarity only glimpsed in some adults. Imagine all of that in a seven-year-old, who ran like any child and played, all God and all boy.

1 John 2:12–17
Psalm 96:7–8a,8b–9,10
Luke 2:36–40

Sunday

DECEMBER 31

• THE HOLY FAMILY OF JESUS, MARY, AND JOSEPH •

*Put on, as God's chosen ones, holy and beloved, heartfelt compassion,
kindness, humility, gentleness, and patience, bearing with one another
and forgiving one another.*
—COLOSSIANS 3:12

Christ has come and our year is done. I feel like the storyteller at the end of old tales who says things like, "If my story be sweet it is yours to keep. If it be bitter blame the teller not the tale." Or this Native American closing, "My story is done, but it will go on, as long as grass grows and rivers run." And that is true. We are at the close of the year and the close of this book, but the story we've been living together goes on and on, so let us put on love and continue down the road, bearing with and forgiving one another.

Sirach 3:2–6,12–14 or Genesis 15:1–6; 21:1–3
Psalm 105:1–2,3–4,5–6,8–9 (7a,8a)
Colossians 3:12–21 or 3:12–17 or Hebrews 11:8,11–12,17–19
Luke 2:22–40 or 2:22,39–40